WRITING
American Style

AN
ESL/EFL
HANDBOOK

Sydney L. Langosch, M.A.

DISCARD

BARRON'S

All inquiries should be addressed to:
Barron's Educational Series, Inc.
250 Wireless Boulevard
Hauppauge, NY 11788
http://www.barronseduc.com

Library of Congress Catalog Card No. 98-43402

International Standard Book No. 0-7641-0792-5

Library of Congress Cataloging-in-Publication Data

Langosch, Sydney L.
    Writing American style : an ESL/EFL handbook / Sydney L. Langosch.
        p.   cm.
    Includes bibliographical references and index.
    ISBN 0-7641-0792-5
    1. English language—Textbooks for foreign speakers. 2. English lan-
guage—United States—Style—Handbooks, manuals, etc. 3. English language—Rhetoric—Handbook, manuals, etc. 4. Report writing—Handbooks,
manuals, etc.   I. Title.
PE1128.L3378 1999
808'.042—dc21
                                                                98-43402
                                                                CIP

PRINTED IN THE UNITED STATES OF AMERICA
9 8 7 6 5 4 3

CONTENTS

Chapter Seven

Introduction

Preparing an academic paper can be difficult, especially if English is your second language. For one thing, rules for content, formatting, documenting, and communicating ideas differ throughout the world. However, several universities have recently conducted studies of ESL/EFL writers. They report that by the time these students are writing English on a day-to-day basis, they have attained:

- Greater richness of expression
- Tolerance for divergent views
- Varied life experiences to call upon
- Ability to accept criticism
- Openness to new ideas

Over the years, as an ESL/EFL teacher, I began to envision a handbook that would help students from various countries adjust to new guidelines for writing papers for North American schools, and in September 1996, Barron's Educational Series, Inc. published my book, *Writing a Research Paper American Style: An ESL/EFL Handbook*. Now, as a result of continued student and teacher interest, I have developed *Writing American Style: An ESL/EFL Handbook*, which has been expanded to include guidelines for writing paragraphs, essays, and research papers. If you are a student in a North American school who speaks two or more languages, and who finds it difficult to sort out the various rules and recommendations for writing academic papers in American English, this book is for you.

Chapter One introduces you to an overview of writing American English style. It guides you through formal versus informal writing styles and a definition of idiomatic phrases. Chapter One also examines stylistic problems such as redundancy, loose construction, gender-biased language, and tips on how to correct these problems. Another helpful feature is a list of frequently used transitions with specific examples of their use.

Chapter Two introduces you to developing paragraphs and their different rhetorical styles. These skills are required in most of your advanced language classes, as well as other disciplines in high school and college. Or you may need to explain a project you wish to undertake, supply information for a financial loan, and provide a sample of your writing for a job application. These are only a few instances where you might be asked to write a paragraph.

Chapter Three explains the different ways to expand successful paragraph-writing skills to writing essays. It gives you the more traditional forms of essays and the criteria for writing such assignments, as well as strategies for responding to essay questions on examinations in other classes.

Chapter Four presents step-by-step suggestions for writing academic papers that require research from the many sources open to students as well as professional writers. This chapter also discusses plagiarism and explains how to identify primary and secondary sources, to maintain research logs, and compose inquiry letters. Telephone research and personal interview techniques are also covered in this chapter.

Chapter Five points out how to come up with ideas for writing academic papers. This chapter suggests posing journalistic questions to yourself; brainstorming, branching, and flowcharts are illustrated in this chapter. Chapter Five also provides guidelines for narrowing down an idea into a research focus that is manageable for writing academic papers and how to develop that message once you have discovered the main direction for your paper.

Chapter Six takes the writer step by step through the most demanding of all academic papers—writing a research paper. This chapter can help you to understand the difference between essays and research papers. It also includes tips for planning the front matter (introduction, tables of contents, if needed) and the back matter (appendices, works cited, or other bibliographies). Rhetorical styles for the writing of the longer paper are again examined as they relate to the research paper, and effective guidelines for writing bibliographic index cards are provided.

Chapter Seven focuses on computer-based and other electronic-based research. Topics include getting started on the computer, using the Internet, and a discussion of available software. The question of how to evaluate computer sources for their credibility and authoritative status is also considered.

Chapter Eight explores the creation of formal outlines and highlights the two styles: topic and sentence outlines.

Chapter Nine introduces you to several key points about how to document the information that is gathered and integrated into a paper; for example, writing footnotes, endnotes, and parenthetical references are covered. Many times it is necessary to paraphrase material or to supply direct and indirect quotes within a paper. This chapter explains these strategies and offers concrete examples for the writer to follow.

Rewriting papers, at least once, sometimes twice, can make the difference between a good paper and a mediocre one. Chapter Ten reviews revision strategies as well as American English punctuation style, spelling tips, capitalization guides, and other correct usage notes.

All of the chapters include prereading vocabulary lists, as well as follow-up questions and activities throughout. Each chapter ends with a summary of its main discussion points and highlights the chapter's key information.

I hope *Writing American Style: An ESL/EFL Handbook* will be at your side when you write your next academic paper and that it will provide the help you need to achieve your writing goals.

Sydney L. Langosch, M.A.

CHAPTER ONE

An Overview of Writing American Style

If you are a bilingual student attending a North American school, the differences in writing in American English along with the changes in formatting, documenting, and organizing your text place you at a disadvantage. This is because the *writing style* for American English, while similar to that of your native language, poses several problems in making the transition from preparing papers in another language.

When you are writing in American English, it is as if you and the reader are having a conversation. What's more, this imaginary conversation is planned to benefit the reader. One of the key ideas behind an American style of communicating is that the reader gets the greatest consideration.

In 1919, William Strunk, Jr., an English professor at Cornell University in New York, emphasized a reader-oriented style of communication in his classes. He also published a book, *The Elements of Style*, which in later years was the basis of an article in *The New Yorker* by a former student, E. B. White.

In 1972, Mr. White published another edition of Professor Strunk's book with a new introduction and additional chapter by White. The book became an immediate success. In the new introduction, White wrote, ". . . Will (Strunk) felt that the reader was . . . a man floundering in a swamp, and that it was the duty of anyone attempting to write English . . . to at least throw him a rope."*

FORMAL VERSUS INFORMAL WRITING

Clear communication that is oriented toward the reader does not suggest that the language is informal. But neither should the writer use a stiff, formal style. Successful authors today use a conversational but objective style of writing. Such writers may use idiomatic expressions, but not colloquial sayings and slang.

A good definition of American English idioms is that they convey meanings different from those of the individual words that make up the expression. For example, if friends say they are under the weather, the expression has nothing to do with rain or snow. The expression under the weather means to feel ill. Such idiomatic expressions are sometimes acceptable in academic writing and can be effective in direct, reader-oriented prose. On the other hand, business writing is less formal and often makes use of idioms, clichés, and business jargon.

IDIOMATIC EXPRESSIONS

Robert J. Dixson in his book, *Essential Idioms in English,* explains the use of idiomatic expressions thus:

Idiomatic expressions have long played an important role in the English language. In fact, the use of idioms is so widespread that an understanding of these expressions is essential to successful communication whether in listening, speaking, reading, or writing (xiii).

---

*From Strunk Jr., W. & White, E. B., *The Elements of Style*, 3rd Edition © 1979. All rights reserved. Reprinted by permission of Allyn & Bacon, a Simon & Schuster higher education textbook publisher.

Dictionaries can help you with your writing. Various grammar, vocabulary, and spelling recommendations can be found in a good dictionary. *Merriam Webster's Collegiate Dictionary* (Tenth Edition) also contains regular and consistent references to styles of writing (which is American English style) through usage labels.

These labels are included in each definition of a word when it is pertinent. The labels are: temporal, regional, and stylistic. The temporal label refers to the time in which the word may have been used. The label *obs* stands for obsolete and is applied to words that are no longer in common use. A regional label corresponds with geographical areas where the word might be used. And of particular importance for an ESL/EFL writer, labels may indicate whether a word is slang or nonstandard.

Merriam Webster's Collegiate Dictionary (Tenth Edition) gives you word listings for all three. The word *horse* has a number of definitions. One explanation is that this is the word for an animal used as a beast of burden, a draft animal, or for riding.

The word *horse* is also listed as a slang expression for the drug heroin. Yet, *horse around* is given a separate entry in the dictionary as meaning joking, laughing, and pushing each other around.

Another dictionary that is helpful for the ESL/EFL writer is the *Longman Dictionary of American English,* which is an excellent guide for authors in style and word choices or other problems pertinent to the bilingual or multilingual writer.

STYLE CHOICE EXAMPLES

The following examples may help to distinguish the differences in style:

TOO INFORMAL:

It takes a bunch of dummies to make such a racket.

TOO FORMAL:

The disturbance emanated from many sources.

STANDARD ENGLISH:

A lot of people contributed to the noise.

WORDINESS

Wordiness is the practice of adding unneeded words to make a point. Think about how you talk to people. If you only have five minutes before your next class or appointment, and you are expressing an important idea to your listener, you will *not* say:

> What I am about to tell you is of the greatest importance as to how the international community should solve worldwide hunger. I want to get you to consider the following to avoid these mistakes like the plague. Then I will summarize what I have told you.

You are not going to insult the intelligence of the people to whom you are speaking. They trust you. They stopped to listen to you; therefore, you are going to say what you have to say in as few words as possible.

Never write to impress people. Keep your writing clear and simple, and use words that are concrete to make your point.

WORDINESS EXAMPLE

TOO WORDY:

I think the growing of potatoes in Northern Ireland became a major agricultural crop in the 1800s.

IMPROVED:

Potatoes were Northern Ireland's major crop in the 1800s.

NOW YOU TRY IT!
EXERCISE 1: WRITING CONCRETELY

Writing concretely means that you use words that are exact and that describe things that can be smelled, touched, heard, or seen. In the exercise below, there are several places where you can select a concrete word or two to complete the meaning of a sentence. When you have finished the exercise, read it aloud to get the feeling of how concrete words complete the meaning and convey a very clear and effective style of communication.

The (dog/Pomeranian) (1)_____,

a toy breed, did not (attract/get) (2)_____

attention until England's Queen Victoria (adopted/selected)

(3)_____ this dog in 1888. The breed became (noticed/

popular) (4)_____ almost immediately.

(Answer Key on page 193.)

INAPPROPRIATE LANGUAGE

The major purpose for writing is to present ideas and information and to avoid language that is not appropriate or related to the main idea. Using sarcastic and humorous side remarks with colloquial tones distract from your efforts to communicate clearly. Enclosing such remarks in parenthesis does not help either.

You should keep your writing objective free of slang expressions, as well as contractions, and focus on creating a formal tone but not one that is too stiff or pompous. (McWhorter 506).

Guidelines about appropriate language include avoiding swear words, cursing, or vulgar language. If a direct quotation includes vulgar language and this quote is related to your main idea then you should quote the exact words. As a general rule, however, do not use street language in an academic paper, or in business writing, unless you have a specific purpose.

REDUNDANCY

Saying the same thing twice is termed redundant. Any repetition or extra words to make your point is also an example of redundancy. For instance, if you write *first-priority* you are repeating yourself. It is more effective to write either *priority*, if that is what you mean, or write *first*, if that is your meaning. The two words are so similar they are not used together. Another example is *petite little* girl. Either she is *petite* or *little*, but not both.

NOW YOU TRY IT!
EXERCISE 2: CONQUERING REDUNDANCY

The following sentences use too many words to express a thought that could be communicated in fewer words. Use the blank lines below to rewrite your suggestion for a better sentence.

EXAMPLE:

This weather is sultry, hot, humid, awful, torrid, sizzling, but it will not affect the outcome of the tennis tournaments because the players are used to it.

BETTER:

This sultry weather will not affect the tennis tournaments because the players are used to it.

1. My neighbor makes many visits to her grandmother, and sometimes she goes as many as three or four times a month.

BETTER: _____

_____

_____

_____

2. I literally never read that somewhat lowbrow novel, which is in very poor taste.

BETTER: _____

_____

3. The law intern almost always has to work a late, evening schedule.

BETTER: _____

_____

(Answer Key on page 193.)

CLICHES

Using certain terms, metaphors, similes, and other expressions that are overused, hackneyed, and tired does not enhance the academic paper. In fact, clichés put readers to sleep.

For example, when the student in the cafeteria says, "Avoid it like the plague," this is a cliché. It is language that is overly familiar or commonplace. When you write, you want to find expressions that are going to clarify your paper without resorting to such overused expressions.

ESL/EFL writers who are new to the United States sometimes use clichés in an attempt to sound less formal. Clichés seem to give a contemporary tone or fluency to what you are writing, but using them is not an effective way to express yourself. In fact, instructors are strict about clichés and consider their use inappropriate in an academic paper.

LOOSE CONSTRUCTION

Loose construction refers to a sentence that is put together poorly. Perhaps it is too long, uses too many words, and is not concise. To avoid loose construction, the writer must take out any unnecessary words. But there is one more problem: placing words in the wrong sequence. Writing too loosely can confuse the reader.

EXAMPLE OF LOOSE CONSTRUCTION

When a sentence is put together carelessly it may result in loose construction.

LOOSE CONSTRUCTION:

John goes to Chicago because he teaches school there on Mondays and Fridays since he does not teach there other days of the week.

BETTER CONSTRUCTION:

John goes to Chicago on Mondays and Fridays where he teaches school.

NOW YOU TRY IT!
EXERCISE 3: ELIMINATING LOOSE CONSTRUCTION

The problem of loose construction occurs more often in the structure of a sentence. It also involves using too many words.

LOOSE CONSTRUCTION:

It is a known fact that the *Titanic* was making its first voyage when it collided with an iceberg and sank in the Atlantic Ocean.

BETTER:

The *Titanic* was making its first voyage when it collided with an iceberg and sank in the Atlantic Ocean.

To practice recognizing and correcting loose construction, examine the following three sentences. Cross out the loosely constructed words and phrases.

1. It is well-known also that although a huge, luxurious ocean liner, the *Titanic* did not carry a nearly even an adequate number of life boats.

BETTER: _____

_____

2. The newspapers announced that the ship was reported to be very luxurious and completely safe, the safest ocean liner ever built.

BETTER: _____

_____

3. A large group, fifteen hundred passengers and crew, or maybe more, drowned that night in 1912 before rescue ships arrived.

BETTER: _____

_____

(Answer Key on page 193.)

EUPHEMISMS

Euphemisms are words used as substitutions for words that are considered offensive. These substitutions are usually inappropriate. Euphemisms can also result in writing down to the reader.

Examples of euphemisms: writing *discomfort* instead of *pain*, referring to a person who has died as having *passed away*, or people are not poor but *disadvantaged*. Because you often hear or read these expressions, you will find yourself including euphemisms in your writing without intending to. Any euphemisms must be avoided.

GENDER-BIAS

Writing that implies only the male sex is no longer appropriate. The relative or personal pronoun *he* is not used when both men and woman are referred to. Writers also avoid using the possessive pronoun *his* and the reflexive pronoun *himself.*

Some authors compensate for this by using the terms *he/she*, *his/her*, or *herself/himself.* Such usage is awkward and should be avoided. One of the methods for eliminating gender-bias is to change the sentence so that it refers to the plural rather than the singular pronouns. A passive voice can sometimes be substituted but stereotypical words must be avoided. Modern usage now refers to *firefighters* (not firemen). A *police officer* is used instead of policeman. People who carry the mail are called *mail carriers*, not mailmen.

In addition, the use of the pronoun *we* or the substitution of *one* is no longer used in most instances. Again, language is oriented toward the reader. Phrases referring to gender can appear condescending. There is a practical consideration as well. Women are involved in all kinds of occupations and professions. Our language in the business world as well as the academic must be adjusted to accommodate these changes.

ACCEPTABLE GENDER REFERENCES

The following are poor ways to express *he, him,* or *his.* Study the examples of more acceptable gender references.

GENDER-BIASED:	If a young artist is not confident, he can become discouraged.
BETTER:	If young artists are not confident, they can become discouraged.
GENDER-BIASED:	TV anchormen are well paid.
BETTER:	TV anchors (anchor people) are well paid.
GENDER-BIASED:	The rookie policewoman answered the call when the bank was robbed.
BETTER:	The rookie police officer answered the call when the bank was robbed.
GENDER-BIASED:	The stewardess served breakfast to her passengers.
BETTER:	The flight attendant served breakfast to the passengers.

USE OF TRANSITIONS

There is another practice that you can use to achieve a smooth, conversational style. This is the choice of transitional expressions.

For example, it is not effective when handling many points, details, facts, examples, and explanations to move abruptly from one to the other. The sentence length in American-style writing is shorter than other countries. Therefore, a writer strives to direct his reader from one thought to another as gracefully and easily as possible through the skilled use of transitions. These are words that help to connect, modify, and fit together complex sentences and paragraphs.

In Candace Matthews and Joanne Marino's book, *Professional Interactions—Oral Communication Skills for Science, Technology, and Medicine,* the authors list transitional words and phrases that can be helpful. They have been selected to help you write a more polished research paper (Matthews, Marino 107).

TRANSITIONAL WORDS AND PHRASES

IN ADDITION

Example: In addition, the store manager will be present at all special promotions.

FURTHERMORE

Example: Furthermore, there will be no more free candy for children at the doctor's office.

MOREOVER

Example: Moreover, the post office will be open at 7:30 a.m.

BESIDES

Example: Besides, the vice president was unable to attend the meeting.

ANOTHER

Example: Another reason for changing the newsletter is to recruit more members.

FOR INSTANCE

Example: For instance, the newspaper has supported many civic causes in the past.

FOR EXAMPLE

Example: Environmental concerns, for example, have been blamed for higher taxes.

TO ILLUSTRATE

Example: To illustrate my point, the newer materials are more versatile.

SUCH AS

Example: There are many more examples, such as the need for more public school teachers.

IN OTHER WORDS

Example: In other words, the curfew in many cities is helpful to parents who want their children home at a certain time.

THAT IS

Example: That is, you cannot take these two medicines at the same time.

FIRST

Example: First, you prepare the turkey for the oven.

SECOND

Example: Second, you add the stuffing to the cavity of the poultry.

THIRD

Example: Third, you adjust the oven to 350 degrees.

FINALLY

Example: Finally, you place the bird in the center of the oven for three hours or more, depending on its weight.

BEFORE

Example: Before you go to bed, please put the lights out.

AFTER

Example: After you have completed the phone calls, keep a record for your research log.

AT THE SAME TIME

Example: At the same time you do your library research, you can make your notes on your bibliographic cards.

THEREFORE

Example: I will, therefore, expect to hear from you in two days.

CONSEQUENTLY

Example: Consequently, I placed an order for more texts at the bookstore.

FOR THIS REASON

Example: For this reason, I am forwarding my order form today.

BECAUSE

Example: Because tomatoes are so expensive, the restaurant substituted broccoli.

DUE TO

Example: Due to the snowstorm, area schools had to close.

ABOVE ALL

Example: Above all, you must keep from falling behind in your reading.

NEARLY

Example: Nearly 500 welfare recipients came to the meeting.

EVEN SO

Example: Even so, there were many residents who did not attend.

NEVERTHELESS

Example: Nevertheless, the program will continue to be funded.

DESPITE

Example: Despite the stage play's many rehearsals, it was a failure.

IN CONTRAST TO

Example: In contrast to the last presidential convention, this one will be easier to attend.

HOWEVER

Example: However, the number of conference members does not always affect the quality of the meetings.

IN COMPARISON

Example: In comparison to other countries in Europe, France continues to attract Japanese visitors.

SIMILARLY

Example: Similarly, there are many German tourists who visit Italy.

IN THE SAME WAY

Example: In the same way, you can influence a child with consistency and high expectations.

IN GENERAL

Example: In general, the concept of a lesser approach is foolish.

IN MOST CASES

Example: In most cases, that breed of dog has genetic defects.

FOR THE MOST PART

Example: For the most part, General Robert E. Lee was loved by his men.

USUALLY

Example: Usually the receptionist takes incoming calls.

 NOW YOU TRY IT!

EXERCISE 4: FIND THE TRANSITIONS

The following paragraph contains several transitions. Can you identify them?

Have you ever thought about what sort of child you were at the age of ten and how it may influence your present life? For instance, were you an active youngster who possibly liked to play outdoor games? Perhaps you may have been a child who enjoyed reading and other quiet pursuits. In other words, most of us have some recollection of our likes and dislikes when we were a certain age. Memories certainly can influence adult life.

Underline the examples of transitions in the above paragraph.

EXAMPLE OF UNDERLINED TRANSITION:

<u>For example</u>, you could leave your radio playing as an added security measure while you are out.

(Answer Key on page 193.)

SENSE OF AUDIENCE

When you are writing, you must have an awareness of the person for whom you are writing. A conversational tone and short sentences are essential in both business and academic writing.

As you write, you should ask yourself these questions: Do I have a strong sense of the person for whom I am writing? Do I feel as though I am talking to that person through my written words? Do I feel as though that person is understanding what I am writing about?

If you can answer yes to the above questions, then you have achieved a conversational and reader-oriented style of writing.

SUMMARY OF KEY POINTS IN THIS CHAPTER

1. STANDARD, UNCOMPLICATED PROSE IS NECESSARY IF YOU WANT TO REACH YOUR READER.

- ■ *Writing that is too formal is not effective.*
- ■ *Informal writing with too many personal references, slang, or inappropriate language is not acceptable.*
- ■ *Standard English is defined as writing that achieves an academic accuracy without resorting to stiff, unnatural styles.*
- ■ *Business writing demands a more informal approach for the reader.*

2. RELIABLE DICTIONARIES

■ *Merriam Webster's Collegiate Dictionary* (Tenth Edition)

■ *Longman Dictionary of American English*

3. STYLISTIC WEAKNESSES TO AVOID ARE

■ *Wordiness*

■ *Redundancy*

■ *Gender-bias*

■ *Clichés*

■ *Loose construction*

■ *Euphemisms*

4. A CAREFUL USE OF TRANSITIONAL PHRASES IS ENCOURAGED TO KEEP WRITING SMOOTH AND COHERENT.

5. WRITERS ARE ENCOURAGED TO DEVELOP A SENSE OF AUDIENCE.

CHAPTER TWO
Writing Paragraphs

KEY VOCABULARY

(If you are unsure of the meanings, check the glossary.)

Nouns	Verbs	Adjectives	Adverbs
aspects	generate	general	carefully
draft	organize	specific	
sentence	proofread		
topic	revise		

UNDERSTANDING A PARAGRAPH

When we talk to people, we manage to organize our thoughts, make statements, support those statements, and give examples whenever necessary—and all of this is done from the top of our heads. Here is an example of such a conversation between two students in the cafeteria:

"Hi. You look tired. What were you doing last night?" asks student 1.

"I had a terrible night because my neighborhood is too noisy and no one tries to respect other people's rights," complains student number 2.

"What do you mean?" asks student 1.

"Well, there was a party going on in the apartment next door until 2:00 A.M. Then the neighbor's burglar alarm on his car started to go off but no one cared enough to check it out. Then, just as I was falling asleep, around 3:00 A.M., the trash disposal people started their pickups. They rattled the trash cans and talked loudly while they worked."

"Maybe we need more laws to keep our neighborhoods quiet at night."

"No," concludes student 2, "we need to be more sensitive to other people's needs and to take our own steps to help each other get a good night's sleep."

Writing a paragraph based on the above conversation is very similar to organizing the two students' thoughts. When we talk to friends, family, or coworkers, we introduce our main idea. The topic of the conversation: *No one respects each other's rights to a good night's sleep.* This is what we term a "topic sentence" in a paragraph. The rest of the conversation will add the supporting details to that main idea.

Another example:

I think it is a good idea that you are taking your parents to Oklahoma to see your aunt. They have never been on an airplane before and that should be a thrilling experience for them. Your aunt is almost eighty and your parents are in their late sixties, so this may be the last chance they have to visit her. And from what you tell me, you have not been seeing much of your folks since you started community college. Yes, a trip to Oklahoma should be a wonderful experience for all of you.

Here is how this excerpt from a conversation would unfold as a written paragraph:

TOPIC SENTENCE: "I think it is a good idea that you are taking your parents to Oklahoma to see your aunt."

SUPPORTING DETAILS:

1. They have never been on an airplane before and that should be a thrilling experience.
2. Also, your aunt is almost eighty and your parents are in their late sixties, so this might be their last chance to visit with her.
3. And from what you tell me, you have not been seeing much of your parents since you started community college.

CONCLUSION: A trip to Oklahoma should be a wonderful experience for all of you.

The last sentence of the paragraph is a natural conclusion. It is not forced, and it does not present any new supporting details; rather, it provides a satisfying closure to the conversation, or to a written paragraph if these words were written instead of spoken.

NOW YOU TRY IT!
EXERCISE 1: DEVELOPING A PARAGRAPH FROM A CONVERSATION

Write a conversation you may or may not have heard recently in which you can readily identify the main idea. After putting the words that you recall on paper, develop them into a paragraph and write the words below:

_____

_____

_____

_____

_____

_____

_____

(Responses will vary.)

WRITING A PARAGRAPH

To develop an effective paragraph you must make its purpose clear. As a writer, you do this by developing a topic sentence that states the main idea of your paragraph. You then expand your ideas by adding details and examples to support your thoughts.

When a paragraph is meant to stand alone, it often contains a brief conclusion and closure (as in the example earlier in this chapter). If the paragraph is one of several that makes up a longer composition, however, it may not have a conclusion, but will need to flow from one paragraph to the other until the total piece of writing reaches its conclusion.

Just as it is important that the writer makes clear what the paragraph is about in a topic sentence, the author carefully plans supporting details that clarify, supply additional information, and provide proof for your writing.

The following paragraph was written by William Strunk, Jr. in his book, *The Elements of Style*. It is a good example of a perfectly written paragraph:

Vigorous writing is concise. A sentence should contain no unnecessary words, a paragraph no unnecessary sentences, for the same reason that a drawing should have no unnecessary parts. This requires not that the writer make all his sentences short, or that he avoid all detail and treat his subject only in outline, but that every word (should) tell.*

WRITING FROM GENERAL TO SPECIFIC

Before you write a paragraph you must organize your ideas so that the reader may follow them easily and with sufficient understanding. One of the ways to do this is to order your main points from the general to the specific. A very brief but clear illustration of this technique is a famous quotation from one of President John F. Kennedy's speeches. The words take the reader from the *general* to the *specific* in only one sentence.

Ask not what your country can do for you, but what you can do for your country.

If we are to analyze this sentence, we can see that it is not only very appealing prose, with a special inversion to set off the rhetoric, but it also moves from the general—*your country*—to the very specific—*what you can do for your country*.

WRITING FROM SPECIFIC TO GENERAL

In his article appearing in *Smithsonian* magazine, author and scientist Henry Genthe wrote,

---

*From Strunk Jr., W. & E. B. White, *The Elements of Style*, 3rd Edition. © 1979. All rights reserved. Reprinted by permission of Allyn & Bacon.

In the sea, sponges sit on rocks, reefs and wharf pilings, showing off bizarre forms and bright colors. Tiny red vases and clusters of brown-gray elephant ears could easily grace the halls of a Beverly Hills art gallery. While they are spectacular visually and chemically, however, sponges are the simplest multicellular beast of the animal kingdom.

Henry Genthe

Smithsonian, August 1998

The paragraph illustrates how writing from specific to general can be effective as well as a welcome variation when working on a longer paper. Notice how both styles reflect the critical thinking skills of deductive reasoning (from general to specific) and inductive reasoning (from specific to general).

PATTERNS FOR WRITING A PARAGRAPH

Most academic papers such as essays, research papers, and reports, and their paragraphs fall into at least one or more rhetorical modes. The most frequently used modes for this writing are informative and persuasive, but there are other rhetorical styles that are used in serious writing and scholarly paragraphs. More often than not, rhetorical styles are combined in longer papers. In a paragraph, there are usually only one or two patterns of development at the most.

DESCRIPTIVE PARAGRAPHS

Paragraphs that appeal to the senses are placed into the category of descriptive writing. This writing uses images, metaphors, idioms, and other choices of words that appeal to visual, auditory, olfactory, touch, and kinetic senses.

EXAMPLE OF A DESCRIPTIVE PARAGRAPH

The wolverine, though smaller than many of its adversaries, can overcome animals much larger than itself such as reindeer or caribou, and drive away other competitors. For example, a wolverine's jaws are so strong that it can crush the much larger caribou's bones. Its large, flat feet are like snowshoes. This enables the wolverine to chase large-hoofed animals through deep snow to make the kill.

NARRATIVE STYLE

Narrative writing tells the reader what has happened or what is actually happening at the time of the reading.

EXAMPLE OF A NARRATIVE PARAGRAPH

A woman looks into the mirror and studies her hairstyle. She decides she must make an appointment soon to have it cut. A man looks into a mirror, studies his hair, combs it, and rearranges it. But he is not thinking about his next haircut. He is worried about going bald.

COMPARISON–CONTRAST

A comparative paragraph deals with similarities. A paragraph that sets up contrasts points out differences. Writing that points out both similarities and differences, side by side, is a comparison–contrast paragraph.

EXAMPLE OF COMPARISON-CONTRAST

Earlier cylindrical vessels, later named submarines, were powered by a steam engine and had to stay on the surface of the water, but it soon became evident that these vessels were perfect for underwater travel. The first submarines were put to use in the United States in 1865 during the Civil War. These basic submarines could submerge just below the surface carrying ninety pounds of gunpowder. They could stay underwater for two to three hours. Present-day nuclear submarines are able to stay underwater for months on end. They are issued an undetermined number of torpedoes that are capable of traveling hundreds of miles to a target.

CLASSIFICATION

Writing that involves classification might also be called division. This development of a paragraph is sometimes called for in special assignments, as in a botany class or a music appreciation class. Other art forms often require writing that is mainly classification. Below we have a paragraph written about the different sections of a symphony orchestra.

EXAMPLE OF CLASSIFICATION

If you are a music lover, you may be able to divide an orchestra into the three different kinds of instruments—wind, percussion, and stringed. The audience is able to identify a piccolo player as a member of the wind instrument section, and will recognize the sounds that come from the stringed section as violins, violas, cellos, and contrabasses. And when a loud crash of the cymbals punctuates an important part of the recital, the listener will identify that player as a part of the percussion section.

CAUSE AND EFFECT

This style of writing requires that an event or a development follow a given circumstance. If the writer is working on a paper about the weather phenomenon known as El Niño, there would need to be a short treatment or history of El Niño with its recurring weather patterns. The results of the storm patterns follow, which is, of course, the effects of the event.

Such a paragraph or essay may be carried even further into a persuasive ending. For example, in the wake of a terrible tornado, the writing mainly is cause and effect. The ending may then switch to an appeal for donations to help the victims of the calamity, which is persuasive.

EXAMPLE OF THE CAUSE AND EFFECT PARAGRAPH

The excessive rains from El Niño have resulted in crop failures throughout the United States. The price of certain produce foods rose to astronomical proportions. For example, many varieties of lettuce (such as romaine or iceberg) doubled in price when this fragile crop was beaten to the ground after days of driving rain, the result of El Niño.

DEFINITION

The mode of writing paragraphs of definition is finding and explaining situations, terms, words, phrases, logos, or anything that can be defined.

There are three types of definition writing:

1. Synonym
2. Class
3. Negation

How many times have you read articles or heard speeches that begin, "If you check the dictionary, . . ."? You have probably encountered the phrase many times.

To write a paragraph of definition is to supply the synonyms for the term. This is followed by sentences that give the subject's distinguishing characteristics. Another way to write a paragraph by definition is to place the article or concepts being defined in a special class.

Finally, definition writing can be accomplished by telling your reader about a certain situation through a negative point of view.

EXAMPLE OF A PARAGRAPH OF DEFINITION BY NEGATION

Today's college student does not fit the usual idealistic, romantic stereotype of carefree life in a higher education institute. In the first place, few of us can afford to be where we are. We cannot expect our parents to pay the full expenses of going to school, and even with grants and scholarships, most of us have borrowed money that will take years to pay off. We must, therefore, juggle our academic pursuits with a series of low-paying, menial part-time jobs in order to meet a part of our expenses. We are faced with rigorous competition for grades, and we are constantly worried that the courses we have chosen to pursue are realistic and appropriate to the job market we will enter when we finally receive our degree.

PROCESS WRITING

Process writing involves telling the reader how to do something. Writing by example is also considered process. When these two styles are combined, the result is a concrete and clear paragraph. This is illustrated in the following paragraph, where both process and example are brought together to guide a reader in preparing herb drinks. The book that this paragraph comes from was written in 1692, *The Good Housewife Made a Doctor* by Thomas Tyron.

> *The best, proper, and most natural way to make all sorts of herb drinks is thus. First, gather your herbs in their proper times and seasons (usually just as they begin to flower) . . . Then dry them in the sun, and put them into closed paper bags; and when you would use them, take such a quantity as you think fit and put them into a linen bag and hang the same in your beer or ale when it is working or fermenting, for 2, 3, 4, 5, 6, 7 or 8 hours, and then take it out.*

PERSUASION AND ARGUMENTATION

Both persuasive and argumentative writing must include clear and suitable supporting details to convince, persuade (sometimes by argument), or otherwise influence the reader to believe, agree, and in some cases to take action.

There are five basic methods of argumentation:

1. Illustration
2. Using facts
3. Referring to an authority
4. Predicting consequences
5. Answering the opposition

Much of our communication in everyday life is persuasive. While we often need responses, we may not always persuade for results only.

EXAMPLE OF A PERSUASIVE PARAGRAPH

In July, 1997, an editorial about Ernesto Zedillo's place in history appeared on *The New York Times* editorial page. As with all editorials, the author is not revealed, but the writing is nearly always persuasive.

> Now that Mexicans have made clear their enthusiasm for democracy, President Ernesto Zedillo must determine how he will govern in the remaining years of his presidency. He can defend the privileges of the remaining powers of the Institutional Revolutionary Party . . . or he can make a clean break with the party's old guard and align himself squarely with the new, more democratic order he helped to create.
>
>

The New York Times
Sunday, July 27, 1997

NOW YOU TRY IT!
EXERCISE 2: WRITING A PROCESS PARAGRAPH

In the spaces provided following this exercise, write a process paragraph; that is, write about how to do something such as how to make a bed, how to study for an examination, or even the directions for how to come to a party. All of these are process topics.

_____

_____

_____

_____

_____

_____

_____

_____.

(Answer Key includes suggested responses to this exercise on page 194.)

SUMMARY OF KEY POINTS IN THIS CHAPTER

1. WRITING EFFECTIVE PARAGRAPHS IN

- *Applications*
- *Tests*
- *Explanations of projects*
- *Academic writing*

2. VARIOUS STYLES OF PARAGRAPHS, ESSAYS, AND OTHER WRITINGS

- *Informative*
- *Persuasive*
- *Comparison/Contrast*
- *Descriptive*
- *Illustrative*
- *Definition*
- *Narrative*

3. AN EFFECTIVELY WRITTEN PARAGRAPH CONSISTS OF TWO BASIC ELEMENTS

- *Topic sentence that includes the main idea.*
- *Supporting details consisting of facts, examples, illustrations, clarification, statistics, and other explanations.*

4. A GOOD PARAGRAPH IS ORGANIZED AND LOGICAL

- *A paragraph can be written from the general to the specific.*
- *A paragraph can be written from the specific to the general.*
- *Chronologically developed papers, order of importance, and spatial order also give a paragraph logic and coherence.*

CHAPTER THREE
Writing Essays

KEY VOCABULARY

(If you are unsure of the meanings, check the glossary.)

Nouns	Verbs	Adjectives	Adverbs
connotation	admonish	accurate	entirely
cue words	collaborate	eminent	farther
essay	endears	general	simply
formula	investigate	systematic	truly
genius	observe	traditional	
humanities	validate		

DEVELOPING AN ESSAY

The essay is similar in structure to a paragraph. Each type of composition has an introduction, a body, and an end. If you can write an effective paragraph, you can write an outstanding essay.

HOW TO WRITE AN ESSAY

An essay is essentially a short composition made up of a series of paragraphs. Its length may run as few as four or five paragraphs, or it may consist of several pages.

A paragraph has a topic sentence that focuses on a main idea and is followed with supporting detail. The essay follows a similar plan except that it has multiple paragraphs with a stronger conclusion.

Essays are among the oldest forms of writing and appeared hundreds of years before the novel and short story. They are nonfiction; most instructors expect the traditional form or style of essay writing. It is organized as follows:

INTRODUCTION: one paragraph that introduces the essay's main idea.

BODY: usually, three or more paragraphs that sustain the idea, support it, clarify, and present details.

CONCLUSION: The conclusion is always included in the final paragraph. It reiterates or summarizes the points of the essay while also drawing a conclusion. Sometimes the final paragraph is only a few sentences, while other concluding paragraphs are lengthier in order to make the important ideas come together to a strong conclusion. Never add new ideas that have not been developed earlier in the essay.

NOW YOU TRY IT!
EXERCISE 1: PLANNING AN ESSAY

If you were asked to write an essay describing an ideal job, you would need to jot down a few ideas before you write. Brainstorming would be next. What interests you most? Name some ideal places where you would want to work, the hours, and of course, a possible salary. You might want a job that would help other people, or you might envision a job that appeals to your creative talents. Arrange these thoughts into an introduction, body, and conclusion. When you complete this exercise, it could serve as a rough outline for your actual writing of such an essay.

INTRODUCTION: _____

_____

_____

BODY: _____

_____

_____

_____

CONCLUSION: _____

_____

_____

_____

(Answer Key includes suggested responses to this exercise on page 194.)

TYPES OF ESSAYS

The word *essay* has several connotations. For example, when you take an examination that includes an essay question or one that is made up entirely of such questions, the use of the word *essay* is quite different from an assignment in a literature class.

In the case of an examination, you are not necessarily being asked to write an essay in the traditional form with at least five or six paragraphs; however, writing effective answers in an essay style can be a major asset in any academic class. For one thing, in the essay question, it is up to the writer to reveal knowledge about the general subject. It is an opportunity to excel. Always respond without hesitancy and with confidence. This does not mean that you should fake answers, but most instructors will give the test taker credit for trying. Always answer each essay question, but if you want to make top grades, you must be prepared for the examination.

There are several strategies for taking tests and writing that winning essay on the exam.

- <u>Organize</u> your writing along a clear idea, but plan it according to the question and the time allotted.
- Always state this focus in a short, succinct thesis statement early in the essay answer.
- Reread the question after writing the thesis statement to be sure that it is answering the question posed by the instructor.
- Plan the remainder of your answer in a one- to two-minute outline. Words listed can be sufficient; just be sure you know where you are going in your writing.
- Always include examples to support your thesis. Usually, two or three are enough, but one will do if time is tight.
- Stick to the subject of your essay response. This is the point where you must refrain from any attempt to impress your instructor. In a classic TV program, two police officers, who are questioning a witness, request, "Just give me the facts." Support general statements with specifics whenever possible, such as the facts, background information, examples, and other supporting details.

■ If you can think of one fast enough, give your ending a brief but positive conclusion. If you can't think of one, do not waste time; just stop writing and go on to the next questions.

WHO ARE THE BEST WRITERS?

In her book published by the Modern Language Association, *Helping Students Write Well* (MLA, 1982), Barbara E. Walvood observes, "The race goes not to the swiftest writers, but to those who best organize and present what they know."

If you are taking an essay test that has more than one question, it is extremely important that you give yourself enough time. But before you do that, be sure to read *all of the essay questions before you begin to write*. Now divide your time according to the questions. If all the questions are equally difficult (or easy), divide them equally. For example, if an essay test allows two hours for four questions, allow a half-hour for each question.

Before you begin to write, reread each question and underline any important words that you will want to pay particular attention to when you write. Some examinations include helpful suggestions, but do not respond to every clue. From your preparations, you must decide which are the most important points of the question.

Finally, after these few minutes of preparation, begin with the first questions, and write through to the last question. There are those test-takers who do not always attack their questions sequentially. As both a writer and an instructor once said, "Take each question, one at a time, write your best, and finish on time." Never ignore or omit one of the essay questions. If you feel particularly strong in an area of one question, perhaps you would be justified to add a little more time to that question.

When an instructor or proctor asks for questions at the beginning of the exam, respond quickly with any query, even the simplest ones. Later in the test it may be too late to ask any more questions.

In many instances, a test may be given by a special proctor who may not be prepared to answer any questions. Do not let this worry you. Simply prepare for any examination as thoroughly as possible. You may even come to like essay questions better than the usual short-answer tests.

UNDERSTANDING CUE WORDS IN ESSAY TESTS

Cue words in essay tests are words that give the writer instructions and directions. Knowing major cue words can make the difference between succeeding and failing an examination. Here are several important words in alphabetical order.

- **Analyze:** Break down the information into parts and discuss these parts: *Define and analyze the different purposes of the United Nations.*

- **Clarify:** This term usually means to further explain and clear up any possible misunderstandings. Often, clarification can depend upon further examples of the original theme: *Clarify the commitment of the nations belonging to the National Atlantic Treaty Organization.*

- **Compare and Contrast:** Instructors use this phrase when a discussion of similarities and differences is needed: *Compare and contrast the business terms* production *and* distribution.

- **Define:** This cue word calls for the writer to give a definition of a term or a situation. It is particularly important to include an example when defining: *Define the* Dow Jones Industrials.

- **Describe:** When asked to describe on an essay examination, it means to explain, to point out salient features of a special occasion, object, procedure, or event: *Describe Europe's political disarray following the Great War of 1911–1917.*

- **Discuss:** If there is an overused term by writers of essay tests, *discuss* is it. The meaning is usually vague, so the test-taker can take some leeway with this question. Discuss usually means to evaluate, to give an opinion on certain possibilities.

- **Evaluate:** This is a term meaning to give your opinion. It is most important to substantiate this opinion with at least one or two important examples: *Evaluate Napoleon Bonaparte's use of artillery in France's famous invasion of Russia in the nineteenth century.*

- **Explain:** Be especially careful with this one. Do not confuse explaining with describing. This actually means to give the reasons behind something: *Explain the discovery of the light bulb and its importance in today's world.*

- **Illustrate:** Give examples: *Illustrate the use of a Breathalyzer test in establishing the inebriation of an automobile driver.*

- **Interpret:** This term is often used when the writer's point of view is needed. Although a wide range of ideas can be used here, do not overlook giving solid reasons behind your opinions.

- **Justify and Prove:** These terms are often used with scientific questions. They allude to validating or correcting a statement or situation: *Justify curbing the use of force in penal institutions and providing rewards for good behavior.*

- **Relate:** Show the relationships or connections between situations. Always give some kind of proof or justification for these relationships: *Relate the incidence of women beginning labor during a full moon.*

■ **Summarize:** This means to briefly review and write a synopsis of story lines and their significance: *Summarize the impact of the Catholic Church on European fine arts.*

■ **Support:** Defend a certain point of view or course of action: *Support the use of the atomic bomb during the final stages of World War II.*

WRITING FOR THE HUMANITIES

It is sometimes difficult to write a paper for classes other than English because the goals are quite different from a language class where the main criteria for the paper revolves around the writing process. In a humanities course, you will be asked to investigate, observe, and write about a variety of subjects.

Another important requirement for writing for courses other than English is that you must refer to ideas and opinions from other scholars. These ideas must then be attributed to the original writer and researcher (see Chapter Nine for documentation guidelines).

The principle subject matter of a humanities course is directed toward the human condition. For example, courses in the humanities are seeking the unbiased, unemotional exploration of human concerns. The main purpose of these papers can be described as informative or persuasive. At other times you will be asked to analyze and review assigned subject matter. Except for answers on examinations in essay form, these longer papers are expected to contain secondary sources.

In many of the humanities courses you will be asked to do an analysis, keeping in mind various rhetorical styles. These will be patterns you may rely on for effective writing strategies. In many instances, longer writing assignments can be viewed as *long* essays. They must have effective introductions that state the main thesis as soon as possible. It is then followed by several paragraphs that will support, illustrate, compare, explain, and give credence to a main idea.

Finally, in writing an essay examination response, you should focus on writing a strong conclusion that will review and summarize its purpose. It is wise to refrain from introducing new thoughts or theories or facts in the conclusion.

WRITING FOR THE SCIENCES

While writing for the humanities focuses on the human condition, science observes the area of natural phenomena, and after extensive investigations, explains such discoveries. Technological courses also adhere to systematic studies of natural and man-made phenomena.

Students in the sciences are often engaged in acquiring more facts and must employ objective strategies for their studies; however, scientists must communicate their findings in a series of papers and successfully respond to essay questions on tests.

Accuracy is especially important in scientific writing. A student must learn to replicate steps in an experiment and to then relay this information in a paper.

Consistency is therefore another important quality needed in the writing of the scientific paper, and since science usually pays more attention to the results of certain experiments than the scientist who conducts it, it is even more important that the writer develop an objective style of writing.

Special formats are provided for the scientific writer, but the elements of a good writing style are still important. For example, the scientific writer must be all of the following.

- Accurate
- Clear
- Concise
- Concrete
- Brief

Most of all, the scientific writer must be able to present extremely complex material as simply and directly as possible. It is often necessary to support one's writing in a science course with a series of graphs, tables, charts, and diagrams. The rules for this usage are often found in special resources provided by your instructor. Should you wish to investigate some of these handbooks on your own, the American Psychological Association (APA) in Washington, D.C. (www.ada.org) has published a fine book that will help you.

COLLABORATIVE WRITING

Finally, in most language classes, you are seldom asked to write as a team, but in the sciences, business management, or social sciences, you are often required to participate with several other students in a collaborative project.

For example, in a marketing class, you and your classmates may be asked to design a new product, research the marketing of your product, and write a report incorporating all of the ideas and research accomplished by your group.

One caution: Never begin to work with another student without first talking to your instructor. In fact, even if you have your teacher's permission, a very organized way to arrange this is to put your partner's ideas and yours on paper and keep a copy of the proposal so that at the last minute your intentions are not misunderstood.

Most of the time, however, you will be assigned by that teacher to another person or group of people to work on the project together. The instructor may at the same time assign to each of you a special role or task, but if not, you and your group should immediately divide the work and cooperate in every way with the other teammates.

The writing task should be approached in the same way—as objectively and systematically as possible. While one's own feelings are important to the direction of the writing, emotional appeals and other extremes are not appropriate in the rhetorical style of American English writing. Each of you must plan your writing, photocopy all material so that everyone has the same material, begin by preparing an overview for each of you, and decide how best to do the necessary research.

Finally, in the actual writing, you usually can pull together the final presentation into one paper. The actual editing and revision can be shared, as can the early writing. Use this book, or another reliable handbook, as your guide so that your group can work together in the most agreeable way.

Collaborative writing takes a lot more time than working singly; therefore, the instructor often gives you and your team members several weeks to complete your work. The problem could be that you or other members of your group will delay working on the project until the last minute. If you encounter such a problem, talk to the instructor.

When the time comes to evaluate the project, it is too late to explain to the instructor that your group had trouble getting started. Always approach any problems first with your group, but if you are unable to get a consensus of thought, then ask the instructor for help.

While there are a number of things that can go wrong in collaborative assignments, some of your most satisfactory and successful work in advanced courses can be a job shared and well executed to the finish.

SUMMARY OF KEY POINTS IN THIS CHAPTER

Essays and paragraphs have similar structures.

1. DEVELOPING AN ESSAY AND A PARAGRAPH

■ *Each needs an introduction, a body, and a conclusion.*

■ *Research is sometimes necessary to uncover new facts, illustrations, and other supporting details.*

2. PATTERNS FOR WRITING ESSAYS

■ *Illustration*

■ *Description*

■ *Process*

■ *Definition*

■ *Comparison/contrast*

■ *Classification*

■ *Persuasion*

3. THE ESSAY TEST QUESTION

■ *How essay questions on examinations are like a literary essay*

■ *How essay questions are different from essays*

CHAPTER FOUR

Writing a Research Paper

KEY VOCABULARY

(If you are unsure of the meanings, check the glossary.)

Nouns	Verbs	Adjectives, Adverbs
draft	access	compelling
focus	argue	journalistic
log	brainstorm	persuasive
microfiche	branching	stilted
microfilm	communicate	
outline	conclude	
research	develop	
text	evaluate	
thesis	investigate	
topic	narrow down	

WHAT A RESEARCH PAPER INVOLVES

When you receive an assignment to write a research paper, do you find your hands perspiring and your heart pounding? Could it be that by writing a research paper, you are going beyond your personal knowledge and experience? Or is it that you are about to begin two separate tasks: researching the paper and writing it in a language other than your own?

In writing a research paper you cannot rely solely on your own experiences. You will need to do the following.

- Choose a topic or issue.
- Explore the topic.
- Narrow it down.
- Gather sources.
- Write a thesis statement.
- Make an argument.
- Present a conclusion.

In other words, you will need to discover outside sources, research them, and study other writers' and speakers' opinions. You must gather information and analyze your findings.

Next you will need to write your research paper. You must communicate your own ideas, but you also must include other writers' and speakers' ideas. In addition, you will need to refer to facts, figures, statistics, and other information from other sources. Therefore, it is your responsibility to document your writing by making clear which ideas are your own and which ideas belong to others. You will need to include information about where you found certain records or statistics. All of this must follow special rules for documenting sources that are not your own opinions, thoughts, or feelings.

DEFINITION OF A RESEARCH PAPER

The word *research*, according to *Merriam Webster's Collegiate Dictionary* (Tenth Edition), is a noun that can be defined as the collection of information about a particular subject. The research process calls upon you to discover and interpret facts and other information. Its purpose is not to just write a general paper on a chosen topic, but rather, to analyze and interpret information while making valid conclusions based upon the research. In many ways a research paper is an effort to answer a question or a series of questions. From this the researcher forms a main idea (that is, a thesis) on which to base the writing of the paper.

WRITING STYLE FOR A RESEARCH PAPER

The writing style of a research paper is called expository writing—that is, it explains and clarifies information. The reliability of sources and the careful documentation of information is important, but a research paper must also keep the reader's interest throughout. Its effectiveness depends on how well ideas are communicated. In addition, a successful research paper depends not only on your efforts to discover interesting sources for your paper but also upon the balance of references you include from outside sources and your own ideas (Gibaldi 4).

PLANNING YOUR RESEARCH

Planning your paper is as important as researching and writing it. As soon as you receive your assignment, you can begin to plan your work step by step. For most writers, the following sequence is useful.

1. Choose a topic.
2. Visit a library.
3. Do preliminary research.
4. Develop a research focus.
5. Narrow down your topic.
6. Write a thesis statement.
7. Write a trial outline.
8. Gather information.

9. Write the paper.
10. Revise the paper.
11. Write a final draft.
12. Assemble the paper and submit it for evaluation.

It is also important that you complete all of these steps in a timely manner. It is helpful to prepare a schedule to meet each deadline (Troyka 603).

RESEARCH PLAN

Decide on a date to finish each step, so that you can complete your paper on time. Although these steps will vary, you will first need to choose a topic, plan and follow through on preliminary research, and then develop a general overview. Finally, you should narrow down your topic and write your thesis statement.

Task	Deadline
Choose a topic	Date
Visit a library	Date
Develop a general overview	Date
Narrow down topic	Date
Write a thesis statement	Date
Send away for material	Date
Set dates for interviews	Date
Gather information (research)	Date
Begin bibliography	Date
Complete research	Date
Write outline	Date

Finalize thesis statement	Date
Write paper (first draft)	Date
Revise paper	Date
Write final draft	Date

Troyka, Lynn Quitman, *Simon and Schuster Handbook for Writers*. 2 e/, 1990, pp. 604.
Reprinted by permission of Prentice Hall, Upper Saddle River, NJ.

KEEPING A RESEARCH LOG

A research log is similar to a diary. When you make a telephone call to ask questions about your research, you should record the time of day and date of your call, the telephone number, and to whom you spoke. Addresses could be helpful later when you need to follow up on specific information. If you send a request by mail or use an electronic means to request material, you should also record this information.

Some students write in their research logs to help organize their thoughts. If you always carry your research log with you, you can enter ideas before you forget them. Do not use the research log for notes from other authors' work.

RESEARCH LOG

The following is an example of notes from a research log. The author of the research paper is writing about television quiz shows.

October 5—Sent a fax to local television station about appearing on quiz show.

October 6—Visited school library to check about quiz shows.

October 7—Viewed movie. Good technical background. Well documented. Notes may be useful for background material in paper.

THE MAIN PARTS OF A RESEARCH PAPER

One of the ways you can refer to the divisions of your paper is to think of them as front matter, text, and back matter.

FRONT MATTER

The front matter consists of the following.

1. Title page: Universities and colleges have special styles for title pages. You should check with your instructor for information on spacing, centering, and use of capital letters.
2. Table of contents: Not all papers require a list of the contents; however, if you must use such a list, centering the heading (Contents) is usually required. All parts of the paper except the title page can be numbered. These numbers appear on the right side of the table. The headings appear on the left.
3. Thesis statement: Most instructors require you to submit your final thesis statement with your paper. It must be stated in one sentence and should precede the outline on an unnumbered page.
4. The outline: You will need to include your final outline with your paper. Instructors ask for this copy so that they follow your ideas and examine the development of your paper.

TEXT

The main body of your paper is called the text. It is sometimes subdivided into different sections.

BACK MATTER

The back matter of the paper includes any notes, reference material, works cited, appendices, and bibliographies as required. If you have written a longer, more detailed paper, then back matter such as endnotes or works cited will be much more complex. However, early research papers will also require a certain amount of documentation that often is found in the back of the paper.

PRODUCING THE PAPER

In most colleges and universities, research papers should not be presented to the professor as handwritten text. You will need to write your paper on either a typewriter or a computer with a word processing program.

If you should be forced to hire a typist, you will need to deliver your work; then, if you make changes while the typist is preparing your paper, you must deliver these as well. Finally, you will not have the convenience of editing your work as you write it. When you type your paper on a computer with word processing capabilities, you can edit the paper as you prepare it. What's more, working on a computer allows you to check your spelling and, in some cases, your grammar.

You really cannot rely on a typist to do this for you. You are quite likely to hear about people who will research, write, and type a paper for a price. This is against the rules of any college or university, and you could be severely reprimanded (if not dismissed from the school). Do not even consider such a choice. It is morally wrong, a financial mistake, and will not give you the experience of doing your own work.

COMPUTER-PRODUCED PAPERS

Writing your paper on a computer is easier than you think. And if you do not own a computer, most universities and colleges have well-staffed computer laboratories for student use. You can arrange with the staff to help you learn to use the computer. Your instructor will have information about these on-campus facilities.

Another choice is to rent a typewriter for the time you will need to prepare the paper. Again, your school will help you with this information. Often the student bookstore can explain the rental of machines and where you may get one.

Also, there are many commercial copy centers with computers on the premises. You will be charged by the hour, but these centers offer a comfortable place to work. Some of them are open twenty-four hours a day. If you have a problem with your schedule and cannot access the computers at your school's learning centers, then you could go to one of these copy centers. There you can do all of your work, and if you are well-organized, you can copy your written material to a computer, print it, make extra copies, and leave the store with your research paper ready to hand in. There are usually free office supplies available, along with other office equipment such as staplers, three-hole punches, tape, and glue. Because you are paying for the computer by the hour, you will not be likely to waste your time.

PHOTOCOPY THE PAPER

Finally, remember that when you submit your paper for evaluation you may not see it again for a long time. In fact, do not be surprised if some instructors do not return research papers. This means that it is doubly important to photocopy your paper before handing it in. It is possible that several people will read your research paper. Of course, your instructor will be one of them and evaluation of the paper is done by the instructor. However, there are assistant readers in some departments who may also evaluate your work. Many schools place research papers on file in the library once they are completed.

TALK TO YOUR INSTRUCTOR

It is absolutely necessary that you talk often with your instructor. You must check at least every two weeks to make sure your work is moving in the right direction. A student, friend, or relative cannot give you information about the research paper. Only the instructor can give you correct answers and the best advice.

After you have studied your course assignment sheet, ask the instructor for an appointment to go over things with you. If you are an ESL/EFL student in a mainstream class, you may want to let your instructor know this.

QUESTIONS TO ASK

1. How will this research paper be graded?
2. Are there any examples of research papers that I can examine?
3. Are there particular topics to avoid?
4. If you are a new student to the class, make sure there are no unusual procedures you should know.

WRITE YOUR PAPER IN ENGLISH

It may be tempting to begin your research and to write your notes in your first language. In fact, some ESL/EFL students write papers in another language. This is a decision that instructors and staff will advise you against. The time lost in working between two or more languages can never be recovered. You will most likely end up with a paper that has a stilted style of writing and it will also lack the nuances of a paper that is researched and written in English from the beginning.

STYLE GUIDELINES

The three major styles used for research papers are based on recommendations by the Modern Language Association (MLA), the American Psychological Association (APA), and the University of Chicago Press. Many schools will provide their students with style sheets based upon these recommendations.

STYLE SHEETS

Should the format of a paper follow style sheets provided by the school and your instructor? Always study the style sheets provided by your instructor and if the choices offered are not clear to you, clarify them. Then follow the rules exactly.

APPEARANCE OF PAPER

It is important to think about the overall appearance of your work. Use only the best bond paper to type on. Do not use any color but white, and be sure that you do not staple the paper, fold it, or leave stray marks or smudges on it. Never make pencil or ink corrections; the liquid whitener that is sold to make corrections is not acceptable. Remember, your paper will be available to many readers. It is not just a communication between you and your instructor, and its presentation should reflect this.

CHOOSING A TOPIC

Deciding what to write about can be the hardest part of preparing a research paper. If your instructor asks you to choose your topic, there are several ways you can make the job easier.

To begin with, you often know a lot more than you think. For example, a writer's experiences in living, studying, or working in another country can provide many compelling ideas for a topic on which to write a research paper.

INFORMATIVE OR PERSUASIVE?

When you write an informative paper, you are mainly presenting facts and explanations. That is, you are not trying to change the reader's point of view.

A persuasive paper, however, attempts to influence the reader's opinions. Its purpose is to introduce a thesis and support it with your own ideas and those of others in order to change the reader's point of view.

If you are not certain about the type of paper you are to write, ask for clarification before you begin your research. Do not wait until you are ready to write your paper. You need to select your paper's supporting documentation while you are gathering material.

EXAMPLES OF INFORMATIVE TOPICS

1. Reducing waste products
2. Lowering cholesterol levels
3. History and purpose of the United Nations
4. Countries to consider for business ventures
5. Computer technology and its use in underdeveloped countries
6. The history of acupuncture

EXAMPLES OF PERSUASIVE TOPICS

1. We must reduce waste products throughout the world.
2. The need to test the average patient's cholesterol level has been greatly exaggerated.
3. The United Nations' chief purpose is to keep peace. Industrialized countries such as the United States and Germany dominate the UN's influence.
4. Beginning a new business in a foreign country can become a high-risk venture.

5. To be competitive, third-world countries need to develop computer technology.

6. Is acupuncture an effective alternative medical treatment?

If your instructor has assigned a persuasive paper, there is one additional method for finding a topic of your own. That is, you can choose a problem; select from newspapers or television newscasts problems considered serious enough to report on but be careful to develop your own thesis from a general topic that you can research and write about.

Instructors sometimes provide a list of topics to avoid. For example, you want to avoid a topic that only has a single source. Do not use one book for all of your examples and supportive documentation. Also, never select a topic that is too broad, such as "The Cause of World Hunger."

Although personal experiences can strengthen a paper, do not choose a topic that is solely related to an event that you lived through. "My Automobile Accident" is too broad and allows you no opportunity to research a more specific, less personal topic. You may use your past experience of suffering a car accident to build a research paper around drunk driving, the present laws, and the various states that deal strictly with drunk drivers.

Finally, avoid a topic that is overworked. Choose an interesting and less familiar research focus and strive for a paper that will be different.

As you plan your paper, you must narrow down your ideas by choosing only the most important ones that will support your writing. Narrowing down an idea is reducing a research focus to a more manageable size. If your focus is too general, your paper will confuse its main point. What's more, you cannot support or document the research focus properly; therefore, you must divide it into more manageable portions.

WRITING A THESIS STATEMENT

Once you have developed the research focus of your paper, you should then begin to write your thesis statement. A thesis statement must be one sentence and only one sentence in which you state what your research paper is about. In fact, a thesis statement is also called a *main idea* in many textbooks, and some schools use this term as much as the expression *thesis statement.*

There are several ways to develop a thesis statement. You may be required to prepare a thesis statement to hand in to your instructor. This step for writing a research paper is very important. Many instructors want to see what you have written so that they can tell if you are ready to move on to the rest of your work.

In addition, if instructors see your thesis statement early, they can give you suggestions about how to improve your paper. When too many class members have selected theses that are similar, the instructor can guide them to another research focus. It is desirable that each class has a wide variety of main ideas from which to frame the work.

The thesis statement gives your paper purpose, but it also points the way to many supporting arguments you will need to complete your paper. Again, you should talk to your instructor as you work so that you can be certain of what is expected of you.

POOR THESIS STATEMENT

1. Capturing wild animals for zoos. (This is not a sentence, and it is not specific enough).
2. Studying in another country is broadening. (Too vague.)

EFFECTIVE THESIS STATEMENT

1. Displaying wild animals in national zoos throughout the world is a barbaric practice that encourages poaching and breaking international regulations.

2. Taking an accredited course of study in a foreign country can be both educationally and culturally broadening.

NOW YOU TRY IT!

EXERCISE 1: WRITING A THESIS STATEMENT

Write a thesis statement that condenses information already gathered in a single sentence. Include both your topic and your point of view for a research topic about college students who are preparing to become teachers. Your point of view is that they should be required to study both liberal arts subjects as well as their major content interests.

(Answer Key includes suggested response to this exercise on page 195.)

TAKING NOTES

It is not easy to take good notes from written or spoken English if it is not your first language. It is impossible to try to write every word as a person speaks, even for the most practiced note-taker; nor can you copy every word if you are examining printed material. These suggestions should help you the next time you take notes.

When you are taking notes from oral speech only:

- Write down key words.
- Include words that are pronounced more forcefully.
- Notice changes in pitch and intonation because they often signal important ideas.
- Listen for nouns and verbs.
- Disregard descriptive words and passages.

■ Watch a speaker's facial expressions for important thoughts, and write those ideas down.

When you are making notes from written information:

■ Look for headings and subheadings.
■ Pay attention to the small boxes (sidebars).
■ Record words and phrases that are in bold type or italics.
■ Note text that is marked with bullets or other special artwork.

BIBLIOGRAPHIC CARDS

Finally, it is time to purchase supplies to help you prepare bibliographic cards. First, you need 3 × 5 inch index cards, because they can be arranged in different ways. A bibliographic card helps you to keep accurate records of your research from the very beginning; otherwise, you might not get to use much of your material because you will not have a record of the source of your information. Finally always number your bibliographic cards in the upper right-hand corner so that they will not get separated.

This information might be kept on bibliographic cards.

1. Authors and authorities in the field
2. Book or portions of books you have read
3. Periodicals you have consulted
4. Any personal interviews
5. Information and quotations from research material
6. Your own notes and ideas about how you will develop your paper

(Number six can be kept on a differently colored card so that you will not forget which ideas are yours and which come from other sources.)

Collinge, William, Ph.D.   The
American Holistic Health
Association's Complete Guide
to Alternative Medicine.
New York, NY: Warner Books, Inc.,
1995.

Once you have completed your research, you may find it convenient to arrange your material according to the three major parts of your paper: the introduction, the body, and the conclusion. However, the essential part of any plan is making sure that it fits you and enables you to proceed with the remainder of your preparation easily and confidently.

SUMMARY OF KEY POINTS IN THIS CHAPTER

A research paper is a form of expository writing that is based upon a thesis supported by facts, figures, statistics, and other writers' and speakers' carefully documented ideas.

1. YOU MUST RELY ON MORE THAN YOUR OWN PERSONAL OPINIONS AND EXPERIENCES.

2. CHOOSE A TOPIC AND EXPLORE IT.
■ *Narrow down the topic.*
■ *Formulate a research focus.*
■ *Gather sources.*
■ *Write a thesis statement.*

3. MAKE AN ARGUMENT.

■ *Select supporting details, facts, and statistics.*

■ *Prepare a working outline.*

4. PLAN A CONCLUSION.

■ *Bring together the main ideas of the paper.*

■ *Repeat the thesis of the paper.*

5. WRITE YOUR NOTES, RECORDS, AND PLANS IN ENGLISH.

6. ALWAYS ASK YOUR INSTRUCTOR FOR HELP.

■ *Schedule an appointment with the instructor.*

■ *Ask questions that will clarify your assignment.*

■ *Find out if certain topics are not acceptable.*

■ *Ask for instructions for style of paper.*

■ *Make sure of the direction of your paper before proceeding with the research.*

CHAPTER FIVE

Coming Up With Ideas

KEY VOCABULARY

(If you are unsure of the meanings, check the glossary.)

Nouns	Verbs	Adjectives	Adverbs
bibliography	brainstorm	concrete	competently
flowchart	focus	critical	effectively
restatement	narrow	quality	
statement	survey	supporting	
statistics			
topic			

COMING UP WITH IDEAS

Sometimes it may seem that you cannot think of a topic and an interesting research focus for an assignment. There are several ways to work through this problem. For example, you can ask yourself journalistic questions. Also, you can brainstorm or use branching to discover a topic. Flowcharts add depth to your ideas.

JOURNALISTIC QUESTIONS

Sometimes asking yourself questions beginning with the letters "wh" can help to develop your ideas. For instance, questions beginning with *who, what, where, when,* and *why* (also referred to as journalistic questions) will help make your research efforts more successful. It will also help you achieve an effective research focus.

EXAMPLES OF JOURNALISTIC QUESTIONS

There are many questions that can be formed with the "wh" words. *How* can also be added to this list. If a writer is planning an informative paper on the use of acupuncture as a medical treatment, the following are a few questions to start with.

WHERE did acupuncture originate?

WHAT is it?

WHO uses acupuncture?

WHEN and how long has it been used?

HOW is acupuncture applied to the patient?

WHY does acupuncture seem to help?

BRAINSTORMING

For students who have not had any experience with brainstorming, the word and the idea behind the practice may be confusing. However, the term is used to describe the practice of writing down ideas as fast as they occur to you, without any special order and without judgment.

Brainstorming is a very effective way to develop ideas. You can use this method to choose a topic or to develop your research focus. First, make a list of everything you can think of about the research focus. You might list feelings, ideas, facts, examples, or problems. There is no need to write your ideas in sentence form. Instead, list words as you think of them. Next, give yourself a time limit in order to keep the process interesting. When you brainstorm, you should not try to judge the quality of your ideas. This step comes later. Finally, reread your list and mark usable ideas (McWhorter 19).

EXAMPLES OF THE WRONG WAY TO BRAINSTORM

YOU:

Who is benefiting most from the North American Free Trade Agreement (NAFTA)?

YOUR CRITICAL VOICE:

I cannot use that. It is not interesting to others.

YOU:

What is NAFTA?

YOUR CRITICAL VOICE:

Cross that out. Everyone knows what NAFTA is.

YOU:

Give the background of NAFTA.

YOUR CRITICAL VOICE:

This is old information. I cannot use that.

Cross that one out. Everyone knows about NAFTA.

EXAMPLES OF THE RIGHT WAY TO BRAINSTORM

Definition
Its history
Acupuncture as an alternative medicine
Benefits
What countries use it most?
Other forms of alternative medicine
Use in the United States
Coverage on medical insurance plans
Training for practitioners of acupuncture
Other medical practitioners' opinions
Licensing
Surgical procedures and acupuncture

BRANCHING

Branching is mainly a visual way of developing ideas. Many writers find this method suitable. To use branching for discovering a research focus, you could select a large paper. Then you will place your general topic in a square or circle in the center of the page. Your research focus is centered and each of your ideas is like the branch of a tree. After arranging your main idea, you draw from that to make room for supporting ideas. These are sometimes called secondary and subsecondary ideas. They are much like the twigs on the main branches of a tree. The circled information is the trunk of your tree (McWhorter 20).

FLOWCHART

The flowchart below is an example of arranging the same concepts in a linear method:

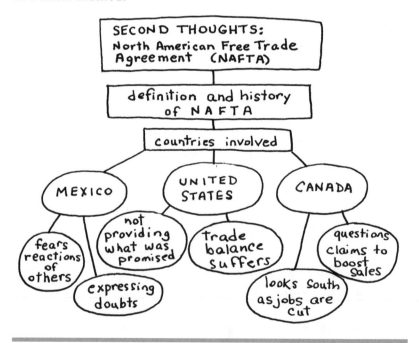

FLOWCHARTS

Flowcharts involve drawing ideas that suggest a certain order of importance or of steps. For instance, if the topic NAFTA is placed in a flowchart, it would progress more or less from a chart with some manner of transition suggested by the placement of the ideas one to another. Once you have arranged your focus in a flowchart, you can use the most important points for subheadings in your working outline, and later, in your final outline.

NARROWING DOWN YOUR IDEAS

At this point, you must narrow down your general ideas for your paper. If your instructor assigned a broad topic about which to write, leaving the choice of research focus up to you, you also need to narrow down the topic. For example, the instructor may suggest the general topic of human rights. However, you must narrow down the topic to find a suitable research focus.

DEVELOPING A RESEARCH FOCUS

Just as developing a thesis statement follows the search for a controlling or central idea for writing a research paper, developing a research focus for an essay or term paper is of the utmost importance.

- State the main idea clearly.
- Use specific language.
- Write your statement in one sentence.
- Avoid using vague, general words.
- Do not introduce new ideas late in the paper.
- Plan your introduction and conclusion for an essay before you write the body of your paper.
- Eliminate any material that does not directly relate to your research focus or to your main idea.

Because multilingual speakers of English have diverse backgrounds, they have more to write about. It is therefore important to choose a research focus and stick to it.

The following is an example of an effective research focus for an essay.

> Knowing what questions to ask when you learn that you must have surgery involving an overnight stay in a hospital can be a matter of life or death.

This statement establishes a research focus about the danger of not knowing about hospital care in the United States. Its specific language—"overnight stay" and "surgery"—establishes the purpose of the essay and the fact that it will give information. The urgency of the writing piques the reader's curiosity with the words "life or death."

The topic also implies an importance of knowing your reading audience. The use of illustrative details will depend upon the familiarity of your reader with the health care system in the United States.

At this point, the length of your essay will not be indicated by the research focus. In fact, with several illustrations, statistical information, and other supporting details, this could easily be a 700- or 800-word essay, or a longer term paper.

NOW YOU TRY IT!

EXERCISE 1: DEVELOPING A RESEARCH FOCUS

You have decided to write a persuasive essay for your English class. Your main idea is that all student teachers should take maximum hours in their subject area, and only as many education classes as are necessary to train the student. In other words, their content area, such as mathematics, should take precedence over method courses.

RESEARCH FOCUS: _____

_____

_____

(Responses will vary.)

DISCOVERY WRITING

After you have tried the techniques of brainstorming, branching, or making up journalistic questions and flowcharts, you may also find it useful to try discovery writing. This step can be helpful, especially once you have formulated a thesis statement.

For some writers, just spending time thinking about what they are going to write is sufficient preparation, but others must put their ideas on paper. This is called *free writing* or *discovery writing*. William Faulkner, the American novelist of the 1930s and 1940s, said that he did not know what he was thinking until he wrote it down. Other writers say that they do their best writing in the shower or waiting at a traffic light.

Discovery writing is a technique for putting ideas down without organizing them or worrying about their accuracy; however, do not think that because you were able to get a lot of ideas on paper, you can submit these early attempts to your instructor. Once you have begun to get words on paper, you will be encouraged to write more, but do not allow your writing to grow "cold." In other words, do not wait to go over it; always underline the best sentences, circle ideas, and make further notes in the margins.

NOW YOU TRY IT!
EXERCISE 2: DISCOVERY WRITING

Set aside five minutes in your work schedule to try your hand at discovery writing. This is how you should proceed. First, select a topic. For example, one of the three following topics may interest you.

1. Your favorite time of day
2. How to save money when you shop
3. Your favorite sport

Having chosen one of the three topics, set a timer or note the time on a clock or watch. Then begin writing. Do not stop writing until five minutes have passed. Do not stop writing under any circumstances. If you cannot think of something, just write, "I cannot think of anything to write" until your ideas start to flow again. When the five minutes are up, be sure to stop immediately, even if it is in mid-sentence.

Should you find this exercise stimulating, try it the next time you are exploring ideas to write about. The one that really interests you will probably keep you writing at a fast pace for five minutes.

DISCOVERY WRITING: _____

_____

_____

_____

_____

_____

(Responses will vary.)

SUMMARY OF KEY POINTS IN THIS CHAPTER

1. **IF YOU ARE HAVING TROUBLE FINDING A FOCUS FOR YOUR WRITING, TRY THESE STRATEGIES TO WORK THROUGH ANY PROBLEMS.**

   - *Ask yourself journalistic questions.*
   - *Brainstorm.*
   - *Branch.*
   - *Draw a flowchart.*
   - *Free write.*

2. **WRITING A THESIS STATEMENT IS NOT DIFFICULT IF YOU FOLLOW THESE SUGGESTIONS.**

   - *State the main idea clearly.*
   - *Use specific language.*
   - *Write your statement in one sentence.*
   - *Avoid using vague language.*

CHAPTER SIX

Gathering Material

KEY VOCABULARY

(If you are unsure of meanings, check the glossary.)

Nouns	Verbs	Adjectives, Adverbs
almanacs	analyze	academic
circulation	circulate	original
citation	document	personal
credibility	interview	supportive
primary research	paraphrase	
quotation	summarize	
secondary research		

GETTING TO KNOW YOUR LIBRARY

Now that you have chosen a research focus and developed a thesis statement, you are ready to gather the information you need to support your paper. In other words, you will need facts, background information, and other authors' opinions and ideas to give your writing strength and credibility. A research paper is built upon other published works by the experts in the field you are researching (Gibaldi 5). In fact, more than half of your paper may consist of material from other sources. However, it is your own particular viewpoint that makes your paper different.

Yet, you must not allow your supportive research information to overshadow your original ideas (Gibaldi 4). It is important to keep your supporting details and documentation in proportion to your original authorship. Your ability to find information, evaluate it, document it in a paper, and integrate it into your writing is essential to the success of your final effort.

Both schools and public libraries are staffed with people who will help you with your search. Do not hesitate to ask for help. For example, you can request information that can be exchanged from library to library either regionally, statewide, or nationally. This type of service is easily accessed through a special computer database. The following terms are helpful in finding the information you may need.

OPEN STACKS

Open stacks are bookshelves that you can visit without the help of a librarian.

CLOSED STACKS

Closed stacks are bookshelves that cannot be accessed by the student.

CIRCULATION AREA

The circulation area is where you check out books, return them, ask for help in finding material, and place a book on reserve. You can also find many other aids that are part of library service here.

REFERENCE AREA

The reference area is where books that are not allowed to circulate are kept. For example, encyclopedias, almanacs, dictionaries, periodical indexes, and other large reference works are kept together.

MICROFORMS

Microforms are photographic copies of newspapers, periodicals, and other special printed matter.

VIEWING MACHINES

Viewing machines provide you access to the library's microfiche and microfilm files. If you learn how to use these viewing machines, you can ask for material that has been preserved on film. Newspapers and magazine articles are often kept on film.

CARD CATALOGS

The card catalogs are indexes consisting of small cards and filed according to either the Library of Congress system or the Dewey Decimal system. However, computer-based indexes are becoming so popular that many libraries are not using card catalogs at this time.

COMPUTER TERMINALS

Many libraries have areas where several computers and printers are kept. One set of computers is used to access material from the library's CD-ROM. Many types of computer information for research are available. Also, libraries are offering their services to students in downloading research onto a disk. The student provides the disk.

INTERLIBRARY LOANS

It can be frustrating to find that some of the sources for your research are not located in your library. However, many libraries can arrange an interlibrary loan by consulting the on-line computer or by placing a phone call (Reinking, Hart 296).

PRIMARY AND SECONDARY RESEARCH

You will need to include in your paper information that you have discovered through your own research. This is known as primary research. An example of primary research would be personal interviews or evidence you have gathered on your own. However, you must document the source.

Other primary research consists of your original observations or investigations. You do not need to document your own thoughts, but you do need to indicate where you gathered your information.

Secondary research is based upon other speakers' and writers' material. In order to include secondary information sources in your research paper, you must not allow any of the secondary research to appear as your own. Always give other authors and speakers credit for their ideas and written material.

EXAMPLES OF PRIMARY RESEARCH

- Personal observation
- Investigation
- Interviews recorded by the writer
- Analysis of historical documents
- Perform an experiment
- Analysis of statistical information
- Audio/visual materials
- Diaries
- Surveys

EXAMPLES OF SECONDARY RESEARCH

- General encyclopedias
- Books
- Periodicals (magazines)

- Pamphlets
- Newspaper reports
- Graphs and other statistical material cited by a previous author
- Newsletters

NOW YOU TRY IT!
EXERCISE 1: USING SPECIALIZED REFERENCE BOOKS

There are thousands of listings in *Books in Print* that provide up-to-date information. You may check for these listings under the author's name, the publishers, or subject matter. Write three pieces of information that you might use to access *Books in Print* in your library. Write the author's name (last name first), the year, and the name of the book or magazine first. Then write a short summary of the subject of the material in your own words.

_____

_____

_____

_____

_____

_____

_____

_____

_____

(Responses will vary.)

PLAGIARISM

There is another reason for keeping accurate and complete notes on your research: to avoid plagiarism.

What is plagiarism? Simply stated, it is making use of or including another author's published work without acknowledging the source of the information. It is using other people's material as though it were your own. Even if you change the original to your own words, this still must be acknowledged as belonging to another author. Direct quotations, ideas shared with you in personal interviews, and videos or audio tapes, must also be acknowledged in your paper so that you can make it clear when ideas are not your own.

Many student researchers write notes in one color of ink for their own ideas and another color of ink for other sources. You may also highlight ideas and sources in different colors. Different colors of index cards are also useful. When it is time to write the paper, you can easily distinguish between your notes and those ideas from a published source (Troyka 609).

Plagiarism is a very serious offense. Copying and referring to other authors' or speakers' ideas can have serious consequences. For example, plagiarism can result in a failing grade or expulsion from school.

In order to keep yourself well-informed on the subject of plagiarism, examine your school's special rules. If necessary, go over documentation rules with your instructor so that you may complete your paper with confidence.

NOTE TAKING

In order to avoid plagiarism, keep notes on the following information from sources you plan to use in your paper.

1. The author's or speaker's full name (check the spelling)

2. The complete title
3. The International Standard Book Number (ISBN), if there is one
4. The page numbers
5. The date and the location of where you found the material

In this way, you can always make an accurate citation within your paper either through the text of the paper itself or at the end of the paper, depending on the method of documentation you selected or are told to use.

The early index cards and/or research log that you keep as you are planning your research (see Chapter Two) is only the beginning. Now you must become more selective and thorough in your note taking.

In fact, one way to tell the difference between early notations on index cards and more detailed research is to use another size of index card. If you change to 4 x 6 inch cards, you will have more space on which to make your notes, and you have the advantage of being able to rearrange them (Troyka 609).

METHODS FOR NOTE TAKING

Some of the methods for note taking that are commonly used by other researchers are summary, paraphrase, and quotations. Also, once you have begun to write, do not forget that you will want to read your notes at a later time, so make them as legible as possible.

SUMMARIZING

One of the techniques for keeping notes is to summarize. In this type of notation, you want to reduce a large amount of material to a few general statements.

In order to summarize accurately, you must learn to condense what you want to refer back to. It is fine to write the work in your own words and to omit the author's words (so long as they are not particularly necessary to the meaning of the text), to abbreviate, and to use some form of shortening certain words, such as using symbols.

Summarizing is also a good method for testing your comprehension of the material you are considering. If you can read the selection and write it in your own words, you can be more confident that your understanding of the material is accurate. This is particularly important for students who speak languages other than English. Should any question of comprehension continue to worry you, ask your instructor to check your notes to see if you are accurate. Once you have confidence that you are summarizing your reference material correctly, you can continue your work with fewer worries.

Finally, summarizing gives you practice in recognizing and expressing in your own words an author's main ideas. The following ten rules will help you to summarize correctly and effectively.

GUIDELINES FOR WRITING A SUMMARY

1. Do not try to summarize until you have read the entire piece of writing. This does not mean that you must read the complete book. If you are interested in a chapter or a subheading of that chapter, read the material that relates to your paper.
2. Write down the main idea of what you have read.
3. List its supporting points on your bibliographic card.
4. Decide on their relationship to the main idea of your work. Make a short note on how you want to connect the research to your own writing.
5. Identify the main points.
6. Condense the main points without losing its essence.
7. Use your own words to condense the message.

8. Keep your summary short.

9. Avoid plagiarism.

10. Write down all facts so that you can document your source when you use it in your writing. Even though a summary is not a direct quotation, you must document the source (Troyka 590).

NOW YOU TRY IT!
EXERCISE 2: WRITING A SUMMARY

Read the following statement from *Business Concepts for English Practice* by Marianne McDougal Arden and Barbara Tolley Dowling, and summarize the paragraph in the space provided below.

What Is Business?

Business is a combination of all of these activities: production, distribution, and sales. However, there is one other important factor. This factor is the creation of profit or economic surplus. A major goal in the functioning American business company is making a profit. Profit is the money that remains after all the expenses are paid. Creating an economic surplus or profit is, therefore, a primary goal of business activity.

_____

_____

_____

_____

(Responses will vary.)

PARAPHRASING

If you are paraphrasing material, you are, in fact, restating very specific portions of a book, article, or other sources. For example, the paraphrase is not only used for written work, but it can also be used when you are doing original research through personal interviews. In other words, you will need to paraphrase or restate the original writing in your own words. Stick closely to the original text when you paraphrase, but put your notes in your own words. If any of your own ideas need to be added to your notes, always indicate this by using parentheses. Better yet, many writers place such notes in another color of ink. If the material is quite lengthy, then it is best to summarize it, not paraphrase it. If it is relatively short, but not appropriate for quotation, then you should paraphrase it.

It is also permissible to change the order of the paraphrase to suit your purposes. That is, if you are making a statement in support of alternative medicine in the United States, then as the writer, you can place the paraphrased material with the most important idea first and the succeeding ideas in the sequence that will best support your paper.

GUIDELINES FOR PARAPHRASING

1. Say what the source says, but no more.
2. Reproduce the source's order of ideas.
3. Use your own words, phrasing, and sentence structure to restate the message. If certain synonyms are awkward, quote the material, but resort to this very sparingly.
4. Read over your sentences to make sure that they make sense and do not distort the source's meaning.
5. Expect your material to be as long as, or possibly longer than the original.
6. Avoid plagiarism.

7. Write down all documentation facts so that you can document your source when you use it in your writing. Even though a paraphrase is not a direct quotation, you must document the source (Troyka 584).

EXAMPLES OF A SUMMARY AND A PARAPHRASE:

ORIGINAL: The 25th day of August, 1751, about two in the afternoon, I, David Balfour, came forth of the British Linen Company, a porter attending me with a bag of money, and some of the chief of these merchants bowing me from their doors.

David Balfour
by Robert Louis Stevenson

SUMMARY: Balfour, arrived London, 1751, British Linen Company.

PARAPHRASE: David Balfour arrived with a bag of money at the British Linen Company in late August, 1751.

DIRECT QUOTATIONS

Another reliable method for citing or documenting your research sources is to quote directly from the author or speaker. For example, a quotation uses the exact words of a writer or speaker. First, though, always remember when placing a quotation on index cards to enclose it with quotation marks. That way, you can easily distinguish your quotation from a paraphrase or a summary.

Information regarding the use of quotations varies among the different styles. The most useful information about using quotation marks can be found in the American Psychological Association's (APA) *Publication Manual,* Fourth Edition, 95.

APA's definition of a quotation is simply this: the use in written form of the exact phrases or words of a speaker or writer. You quote that writer or speaker by using quotation marks for text that is forty or fewer words in length (APA 95).

Quotations that are more than forty words should be placed in block form in which the quotation marks are omitted. When you use a block quotation, start the quotation on a new line indented five spaces from the left and right margins. The material is double-spaced, and it will read as a continuous block until the writer reaches the end of the quoted material.

You should include the author, year, and specific page of the printed material from which you are quoting. If it is an interview, also include a short description of who is being quoted and the circumstances of the interview.

AN EXAMPLE OF A QUOTATION UNDER FORTY WORDS

As the eighteenth-century American journalist, Charles Swain, wrote, "Let tomorrow take care of tomorrow."

AN EXAMPLE OF A QUOTATION OVER FORTY WORDS

Rudyard Kipling, the British author and poet who spent many years in India, once wrote:

> When earth's last picture is painted, and the
> tubes are twisted and dried,
> When the oldest colors have faded, and the
> youngest critic has died,
> We shall rest, and faith, we shall need it—
> Till the Master of All Good Workmen shall set
> us to work anew!

USE OF PHOTOCOPIED NOTES

If you require extensive and exact information in your notes, and you are working with printed material, use a photocopier. Libraries offer this service. Copy the page or pages you will need and always carry a pair of scissors and cellophane tape in your book bag so that you can photocopy and clip the information as you are doing your research. Keep a page without altering it, and clip the information you need at that moment. This may take extra time, but in the end, it will serve you well. Never under any circumstances remove a page or clip a portion of the original book or magazine article.

When you photocopy, always make sufficient notes on the portion you have saved with the book, page number, and author. Also, do not include too much material and always note why you have included it.

Try not to make too many notes and avoid becoming repetitious in your selections. Instead, early in your research, decide what you will record and what you will not.

GUIDELINES FOR REQUESTING INFORMATION

Sometimes you will need to write a letter or send a fax to ask for material for your research paper. Always give yourself enough time at the beginning of your research to receive a reply to your request. Research papers can be enriched by new sources and different approaches.

You do not always need a specific person to whom to send your letter. There are several ways to direct correspondence. You can send it to a department, or to a special area of interest, or perhaps to a more general marketing or public relations department of a business or agency. In fact, do not hesitate to address your letter to the president of a company. You can be sure that any mail addressed to the head of a company will receive prompt attention.

Another way to expedite your inquiries is by using a fax machine, which digitizes and transmits a graphic image via regular telephone lines using modems. However, when faxing an inquiry, it is better to telephone in advance to make sure you have the correct fax number.

Also, always avoid use of a gender salutation such as Dear Madame or Dear Sir. Instead, the letter may be directed to a department or a special area and addressed as such. Second, do not address mail "to whom it may concern." This salutation is seldom used in either business or academic correspondence.

EXAMPLE LETTER OF INQUIRY

555 Pinecrest Lane
Baton Rouge, LA 00000
August 4, 1996

Bell Atlantic
C & P Telephone
800 Van Dam Street
Rockville, MD 00000

Dear Customer Service Department:

I am writing a research paper on drug abuse prevention programs directed to the parents of young children, and I recently learned that your company has published the brochure, *Growing Up Drug Free, A Parent's Guide to Prevention*.

Could you please send a copy of this booklet to the above address as soon as possible?

Sincerely,

Patrick Johns

Patrick Johns

TELEPHONE SKILLS FOR RESEARCH

Using the telephone to gather information for your research paper is an effective way to get material quickly. Telephone research also enables you to do much of your work efficiently and easily from the comfort of your own work space.

Telephone research also adds a great deal of fresh material and a contemporary tone to your paper. The first distinction you must make, however, is whether the person you wish to interview can be identified as an expert. A casual acquaintance whom you have met in the school cafeteria has opinions, but that individual will not have important facts and experience that you can rely on.

GUIDELINES FOR CHOOSING PEOPLE TO INTERVIEW

1. Find a person who has personally experienced a certain event. For example, an adult who served in the military during the war in Vietnam may be considered an expert in the conditions under which the servicemen fought. If asked about the conduct of the war or the political implications, that information would not be expert.

2. Locate any individual who is employed as a part of a firm as their public relations contact. These people are considered expert in that their training is in communication. They are an informed source representing the company they work for.

3. Contact the faculty at your college or another such institution. The faculty at your college might be an excellent source for seeking a personal interview within a certain field of interest that relates to the writing of your paper. An example of this is the instructor who may have spent the summer as a volunteer for an environmental program such as replanting trees after a devastating forest fire.

4. Telephone federal, state, and local government officials. These workers are experts because of their training and experience. Some offices have people trained to provide information and interviews to the public.

Another reason for contacting someone special is that one of these experts may also suggest other valuable sources to contact.

Placing telephone calls, however, requires planning before you dial that number. In order to make yourself easily understood, you will want to make notes before you call. Then, you should be prepared to spell certain words or terms if your accent makes it difficult for the person taking the call to understand you. If you are prepared before you make your inquiries, you can easily communicate by telephone. In fact, most busy professionals prefer talking on the telephone over a face-to-face interview.

Tony Hitt and Kurt Wulff, in their book, *Positive Impressions: Effective Telephone Skills* note that the confidence with which you place your call can also be reflected back to you. For instance, if you begin in a disorganized, hesitant, timid fashion, the person receiving the call will become impatient and will want to move on to the next call.

Any call you make will be competing with other phone calls. Therefore, make a list of the things you want to discuss. Have a goal in mind. What is it you want to find out? Do you need directions, specific information, addresses, telephone numbers, or explanations of terms?

THE TELEPHONE INTERVIEW

There are three main points to remember when placing a telephone call.

First, you will need to have an objective. When the call is completed, what do you want to have gained from the communication?

Second, focus all your attention on the phone call at hand. Do not allow events happening around your work area to distract you.

Third, and most important, have an agenda. Know exactly what you want to discuss and how you want to go about it. Your goal should be never to hang up the phone and say, "Oh, I wish I had asked her about...."

A. W. (Tony) Hitt with Kurt Wulff
Positive Impressions: Effective Telephone Skills

CONDUCTING A PERSONAL INTERVIEW

When you conduct a personal interview, the information you must include in your research notes is the name of the person interviewed (whether it was by telephone or in person) and the date you did the interviewing. Always make an entry in your research log, but at some time soon after the call, you must also write a bibliographic card.

Again, as illustrated in the *MLA Handbook,* an example of the citation used for an interview which you conducted yourself might be as follows:

Pei, I. M. Personal interview. 22 July 1993.

In this case, the interview was not titled, but it was conducted by you.

When you interview by telephone, according to the *MLA Handbook* the style is:

Poussaint, Alvin F. Telephone interview. 10 Dec. 1990. (179).

Interviews on television and radio can also be cited by enclosing the title of the interview in quotation marks. The other information remains the same:

(Name of person interviewed on radio or TV). Interview with
_____, "Title." If the interview does not have a title,
then simply use the word interview (178).

INFORMATION TO KEEP ON BIBLIOGRAPHIC CARDS

Keeping accurate bibliographic cards at this point in your research
can save hours of work as you near the completion of your paper.
Here are just a few of the rules to follow as you do your work:

1. Keep names of companies and individuals in an alphabetical arrangement.
2. Ask for the correct spelling of names and addresses.
3. Check telephone and fax numbers.
4. Make notes on conversation and date call was placed.
5. Keep complete information on the expertise and qualifications of the person you are querying.

ANALYZING AND EVALUATING YOUR SOURCES

The purpose of most research papers is to convey information,
facts, and ideas. Therefore, it is important that your sources are
accurate and complete.

How can you judge the material you wish to use to document
your research paper?

First, you can check the reliability of the book, magazine,
newspaper, or professional journal by finding out how long it has
been published, the organization with which it is affiliated, and
the academic or experiential background of the writers.

If you are interviewing someone for information to use in your
paper, you should consider the individual you will question. For

instance, if you are writing about NAFTA, you will not want to interview a fellow student for information to include in your paper. That is, you will not include any quotations from such a source as factual. But if you do wish to include another person's statement, you can always make it clear that this quotation reflects an opinion. Most of the time, it is a good plan to limit any personal interviews to experts in the area of interest about which you are writing.

As Kathleen T. McWhorter suggests in her book, *The Writer's Express*, there are several ways to test the reliability of a source.

QUESTIONS IN ANALYZING THE SOURCE OF ORIGINAL MATERIAL

1. What is the reputation of the source?
2. For what type of information is it best known?
3. Who is the intended audience?
4. What type of documentation does it provide and does it list sources of information? (285)

SUMMARY OF KEY POINTS IN THIS CHAPTER

Once you have chosen a research focus and developed a thesis statement, you will need to gather sources to back up your paper.

1. YOU CAN FIND FACTS, OPINIONS, AND BACKGROUND INFORMATION

■ *Get to know your library.*

■ *Write for information from agencies, business offices, industries, government offices, and others.*

■ *Arrange telephone and personal interviews.*

---

2. TWO MAIN DIVISIONS OF RESEARCH

■ *Primary sources—These are sources from original materials such as diaries, surveys, and personal and telephone interviews.*

■ *Secondary sources—These are sources of information from books, magazines, and newspaper articles.*

3. NOTE-TAKING METHODS

■ *Paraphrasing—write in your own words.*

■ *Summarizing—reading text and reword in a shorter, more condensed form.*

■ *Direct quotation—use the exact words of an author enclosed in quotation marks.*

4. ARRANGEMENTS AND PREPARATION FOR PERSONAL AND TELEPHONE INTERVIEWS

■ *Pay attention to details.*

■ *Use care in preparation of questions.*

■ *Keep reliable notes for later documentation.*

CHAPTER SEVEN

Computer-Based Research

(If you are unsure of meanings, check the glossary.)

Nouns	Verbs	Adjectives, Adverbs
abstracts	access	electronic
CD-ROMs	browse	imaginary
electronic mail	download	
emoticons		
hardware		
Internet		
modem		
on-line databases		
portable databases		
software		

GETTING STARTED IN COMPUTER-BASED RESEARCH

Imagine visiting your library with no supplies other than a 3- × 4-inch computer disk. When you arrive, you sit down at a computer in a special area for library visitors. There you will find a database on a special CD-ROM (Compact Disc, Read-Only Memory).

When you find the information you are looking for, you insert your computer disk in a small slot labeled "download." In less time than it takes to photocopy material, you can transfer the information you wish to access for your research paper to the disk you have loaded in the computer. Another method for collecting materials from computer sources is to print them on the computer printer that is provided by the library.

Such possibilities for research are no longer imaginary. Now, instead of depending on a few reliable research methods such as examining a book on a shelf or viewing information on microfilm, you can access a vast database of source material through the newest computer technology. In fact, any visitor to the library is often forced to use a computer to access information about books, authors, publishers, and copyright dates because many libraries have closed their card index. CD-ROMs are updated by their manufacturers every few months, while card index files are expensive and time-consuming to keep up to date.

Certainly, printed sources will continue to remain an important method for researching material. What's more, photocopying this material will continue to be a major part of your efforts as you research your paper. But if you are willing to spend some time in preparation, you can learn to use CD-ROMs, e-mail, the Internet, and other electronic sources to gather important research materials. In fact, with the opportunities now offered through computer-based research, it would be almost impossible not to use electronic sources.

However, this chapter is not merely a story of out with the old, in with the new. The reality is, most student researchers successfully combine technology-based research with the more traditional sources such as books, daily or weekly newspapers, magazine articles, and other printed materials.

TYPES OF ELECTRONIC SOURCES

Universities and colleges throughout the world have moved quickly in the past few years to expand their computer technology. They have made such sources easily available to students, too. The following are the major sources of computer-based information.

1. CD-ROMs
2. Internet
3. home computers
4. e-mail

CD-ROMS

CD-ROMs contain read-only memory. They are portable compact discs that cannot be added to or altered except by the original programmer.

The advantage of CD-ROMs is that they usually do not require installation into an individual computer system. Instead, the compact disc containing the information is inserted in the computer much like a selection of music that is used on a CD player. This is the reason that such computer-based resources are referred to as portable. Other nonportable sources are accessed through a network or as part of e-mail communication.

Do not forget, however, you must keep reliable notes after you have downloaded material. Perhaps this sounds difficult and cumbersome after the ease with which you have accessed your other sources. But you still need to transfer material to another computer. Therefore, keeping a good record of your disks is necessary. Then, when you need to retrieve your research and write your paper, you can refer to these notes to make the best use of the material you have gathered.

One way to keep track of disks is to use those same bibliographic cards with shortened notes of what you have saved, whether from the printer or on a disk. Why this extra step? Because you can save yourself time when you begin to write if you have your index cards briefly noted and kept together as one separate file. It is never necessary to take complete notes. Otherwise, using computer-based material will not save time.

Downloading information from CD-ROMs can be especially helpful for people who have a busy schedule. It is hard to find the time to spend at libraries along with classes, studies, employment schedules, and family commitments. Downloading onto your own disk is a great time saver enabling you to use a computer in your learning center or your own home computer. Then you can find the material when you want to write about it.

CD-ROM ENCYCLOPEDIAS

These encyclopedias and dictionaries are now available on CD-ROM.

- *Encyclopedia Britannica CD*
- *Compton's Interactive Encyclopedia*
- *Compton's Reference Collection*
- *Random House Webster's Unabridged Dictionary*
- *American Heritage Talking Dictionary*

THE INTERNET

The Internet is considered nonportable and is accessed through a network of electronically based information available on an extensive network of sources throughout the world. The Internet is a worldwide network of computers connected by high-speed data lines and wireless systems through which you can communicate. Established in 1969 as a military system, it now allows individuals to communicate with corporations, schools, and people who have an e-mail address or a home page on the World Wide Web (WWW).

Internet services combine the use of audio, video, graphics, and text for procuring information. If the topic of your paper is NAFTA, and you have narrowed this down to an update on the North American Free Trade Agreement, it is possible to gather material through an Internet service.

In addition, Internet services offer translations from one language to another. This can be accomplished with a simple click of the right keys. For example, if the original material on NAFTA is in Spanish and the researcher speaks French, the researcher can click on a translation from Spanish to French.

Translations that offer such a choice for a multilingual student, however, might be best accessed in English only. As a matter of fact, many multilingual students find it helpful to read the material first in their native language, but then to click on the English translation while making their notes in English. However, there is an advantage to being multilingual if the material is not offered in English. Then, by all means, use any resources you need.

In order to use the Internet you must have an Internet service provider. To choose one, look for advertisers in your telephone directory yellow pages for more information on how to arrange for these providers. You also may check for providers that do not charge for their services. They are limited in what they provide, but the choice can give you the start you need.

The key to doing research on the Internet is to locate specific information. Because the information on the Internet is so vast, and is always changing, you will want to begin with a *search engine*. To learn about these, work with your computer labs at your school, or inquire at your library.

Here are a few suggestions for accessing the Internet and finding specific material.

1. Be as specific as possible. Let us suppose that you are looking for information about Frederick Douglass, an ex-slave who became a leader in the movement to abolish slavery and a famous nineteenth-century writer. An example for locating the URL, or network address for on-line information is <gopher://gopher.vt.edu:10010/02/73/1>. Your next step is to enter two or three words to aid the search. You might then write Frederick Douglass, abolitionist, 1860. **Note:** It is always wise to check network addresses before each use because they change frequently.

2. Link your terms. Most search engines let you use connectors such as *and, or, not.* If you want to limit your search to Frederick Douglass' work as an abolitionist, you could list your request as follows:

   Frederick Douglass, abolitionist before 1860

3. If your search is too successful: Sometimes your query will result in hundreds of matches. Just remember that the best matches are listed first; you do not have to continue to visit additional sites once you have found the information you need.

FINDING INFORMATION ON THE WORLD WIDE WEB

To access the World Wide Web for research purposes you need software called a Web browser. If you have your own PC, however, you can also access the browser that is built into the service's communication system.

Libraries and learning centers offer this service as well. The advantage of working at a learning center is that you can always find someone who can guide you through the process.

One of the most extensive types of software to consider for a home computer is Electric Library (http://www.elibrary.com). This service offers international news wires, photographs, maps, and many other valuable sources for research. Students who have restricted schedules may find that such software would be most helpful.

It is very important as you use the Internet to keep in mind the thesis of your research. Because it is so easy to gather information, the researcher must not become distracted and spend too much time on material not directly related to the research at hand.

FOCUS ON THE MAIN IDEA

Writers often write their thesis on an index card. Then they place it near the computer as they work. Keep the thesis before you at all times.

If you write your main idea on an index card and keep it in front of you at all times, you can check the relevancy of your material and your thesis statement while the material is still on the screen. Another reason for keeping the thesis of your paper clearly in mind, is that you must use the right terms to find your information in the first place.

NOW YOU TRY IT!
EXERCISE 1: SEARCH WORDS FOR COMPUTER-BASED RESEARCH

Let us suppose that you are writing a paper and you need to explore the locations of houses and buildings designed and constructed by Frank Lloyd Wright, the famous American architect.

Try to assemble several words in advance of your search on a computer for the background information you will need to write your paper.

Here is an example of how you might determine topic words for locations of houses designed and built by Frank Lloyd Wright.

Example: Architecture, Frank Lloyd Wright, houses, twentieth century.

Now practice putting together a few more words or phrases for the search listed above, or for that matter, one of your own choice. _____

_____

_____

_____

_____

_____

_____

_____

_____

The text from a computer-based program is not necessarily the best there is. Remember that nothing guarantees the quality or accuracy of the information from on-line research. You, the writer, must be the final judge.

MAKING CHOICES

Not all of your sources will be spectacular. Often you may choose to use material that is of average quality if it suits your purpose because you do not want to eliminate sources too quickly. Certain text of average interest can become an important part of your paper, supplying you with a piece of information just when you need it.

HOME COMPUTERS AND THE INTERNET

There are cases where the investment in a home computer, along with an on-line service, could be a good decision. For example, you might be a married or single-parent student. Working while you are attending classes leaves you very little time to visit libraries. Therefore, an investment in a home computer and a modem plus a commercial on-line Internet service can keep you competitive in the academic arena.

Home computers with on-line services involve installation and a monthly charge for the use of an on-line service. These charges are sometimes based on time or you may want to subscribe to a service that has a standard monthly fee. If the circumstances warrant it, the opportunities offered by having a personal home computer with on-line services may be cost-effective. What's more, these services can be used in all your courses throughout your college career.

E-MAIL AND HOW TO USE IT

Electronic mail (e-mail) combines the *advantages* of writing with the responsiveness of the telephone. As quickly as the term e-mail was established, the ability to communicate with different libraries and different countries has increased through linking e-mail to an electronic network such as the Internet. All you need to get started in e-mail is access to a computer with the right hardware, the appropriate software, and an e-mail address.

GUIDELINES FOR USING E-MAIL

1. You will need to arrange for an e-mail address.
2. Learn to write e-mail headings.
3. Learn to write the body of the message. You can either write out by hand the message for the person with whom you plan to communicate or you may simply enter the message directly on the keyboard.
4. Users of e-mail often use special abbreviations and emoticons to make their points.

If you are unsure of how to establish an e-mail address for yourself, check first with your university or college. Many schools provide this service to their students. Some schools charge a small fee, but the use of such data is far less expensive than subscribing to your own network with e-mail capabilities.

You may have friends who have e-mail services. They might be willing to let you use their computers for your research if you can find another computer on which to write your paper.

Finally, overuse of e-mail might result in more replies than you can handle. This could be costly because you might have a service that charges per response.

BROWSING

In addition to direct access to one e-mail address for the purpose of researching a subject, you can use some of the e-mail programs to communicate with other e-mail subscribers. There are designated ways to place a notice for several thousand people to respond to. This is hard to control, so if you are concerned about the cost of e-mail, you may not want to use such a broad and far reaching method. However, if you are searching for obscure or little-known information, you may enjoy the results you get from posting a notice on a special e-mail program.

It is important to stress that using electronic on-line research techniques is difficult and confusing in the beginning. If this is your first experience in using on-line research, you may need to find another student or a tutor in a learning center to guide you through your first attempts.

NEWS GROUPS ON THE NETWORK

Many schools, libraries, and learning centers subscribe to on-line news groups. This is a helpful resource for student writers who are researching late-breaking journalistic topics. However, there are thousands of news services covering a huge range of topics. Consult with a staff assistant to help you find a regularly updated list of news groups. Then, choose only material that is related to your thesis. Some topics would not be appropriate for such a search, but if you are writing about an area in which up-to-the-minute current events are helpful or necessary, then it is well worth the time to access such news groups. The staff at a library or learning center can help you to use this important resource.

BROWSING BULLETIN BOARDS

Another possibility when using a computer for research is to make use of the local electronic bulletin board systems (BBS). First you have to put out your message. You can do this on either the Internet or through e-mail. There might be a great response to your call. On the other hand, computer operators paying attention to the BBS are fewer than the other more general e-mail avenues, and the response to your request can be sparse.

DOCUMENTING ON-LINE SOURCES

Sometimes puzzling questions arise once you have gathered material from electronic sources. One of those is quite often the way to cite information that you have retrieved from CD-ROM, the Internet, or e-mail sources.

In general, any material that is available both through printed publications and on-line can best be documented through its printed source only. However, if the source is not easily found in printed material, by all means, document the electronic source by citing the publication medium and the vendor's name, as well as the date of the electronic publication (Gibaldi 152).

If, however, your material is directly from the network and cannot be found in any printed material such as a newspaper, magazine, or book, then you can document it as a personal interview and contact through the Internet. See Chapter Six for examples.

Do not limit yourself, however, to only one method of research. Always integrate your computer-based research with traditional methods for the best results.

HOW TO KNOW WHEN TO STOP

It is a good idea to review your early (working) outline as you are researching. This will help you to know when to stop. Unfortunately, there is no magical formula for the number of sources you will need. You cannot be certain as to the direct quotations you will need to the background material you should read.

Next, review your original planning notes. Check the dead

lines you set for yourself. If you find that you are more than two or three days over the time limit for researching, you may want to complete this step so that you have enough time to write an effective and engaging paper.

Finally, you may sense that you have enough material. If that little voice tells you that you have exhausted the search for materials, then trust your feelings. You are the author. If, on an intuitive level, you can estimate the examples and the backup material you will need for each major section of your paper, then you can be sure you are well prepared to write the final text.

SUMMARY OF KEY POINTS IN THIS CHAPTER

Computer-based research offers a writer new and surprising ways to gather sources for a research paper.

1. CD-ROMS ARE PORTABLE DATABASES NOW AVAILABLE TO PURCHASE FOR A PERSONAL COMPUTER OR TO ACCESS IN A LIBRARY OR COMPUTER LABORATORY.

- *CD-ROMs are useful for background material.*
- *CD-ROMs offer a vast listing of facts, figures, and statistics for research.*
- *On-line research is possible through the use of a modem and access to one of the standard computer lines.*
- *Electronic mail (e-mail) offers an opportunity to investigate special bulletin boards and home pages not available on-line.*

2. COMPUTER RESEARCH HAS CHANGED METHODS FOR RESEARCH. IT PROVIDES THE CHANCE TO SAVE TIME.

- *Downloading information from a CD-ROM or other on-line sources to your own research disk.*

3. COMPUTER-BASED RESEARCH REQUIRES SPECIAL CITATIONS. THESE ARE RELA-
TIVELY NEW AND MUST BE CHECKED AT THE TIME OF PREPARATION.

4. COMBINING BOTH TRADITIONAL METHODS FOR RESEARCH WITH THE ABILITY TO
ACCESS INFORMATION AND DOWNLOAD IT TO ANOTHER DISK IS RECOMMENDED.

5. BECAUSE OF THE ENORMOUS AMOUNT OF COMPUTER-BASED MATERIAL NOW
AVAILABLE, IT IS VITAL TO CHECK ON THE QUALITY AND RELIABILITY OF YOUR
SOURCES.

■ *Make certain that the writer has good credentials.*

■ *Do not use repetitious or poor-quality materials from a computer and always know when to stop by following deadlines and referring often to your thesis and working outline.*

CHAPTER EIGHT

The Formal Outline

(If you are unsure of meanings, check the glossary.)

Nouns	Verbs	Adjectives, Adverbs
acupuncture	digress	accurate
alternative	finalize	chronological
details	indent	clear
division	organize	formal
format	predetermine	spatial
main idea	wander	temporary
outline		
phrase		
subdivision		
subgroupings		
topic outline		

PREPARING THE FORMAL OUTLINE

It is only natural that you are impatient to begin your paper, but preparing a careful guide for your writing is an important step. Your instructor usually requires a formal outline as part of a longer, more complex paper. Here are the reasons you must not neglect this essential step.

- Working from an outline provides a plan for writing.
- An outline encourages you to be more accurate.
- An outline prevents repetition.
- An outline keeps you from omitting material.

BRIDGING THE GAP

First, using your working outline as a basis for the more formal one makes the writing much easier. Lynn Quitman Troyka, in her book, *Handbook for Writers*, suggests that you divide your index cards in the same way you plan to divide your outline. Each division of your outline will then relate to the thesis (main idea) for your paper.

For instance, if you are working on a paper about acupuncture, you may wish to begin your outline with a history of acupuncture. All of the notes you have on the history of this ancient Chinese medicine will go in one group.

Next, the second group of cards are arranged for the next Roman numeral of your outline, and so on. Keep in mind that all of these cards and their piles must relate to the thesis.

Length and abundance of material is not in itself impressive. Therefore, your paper must move smoothly from one point to another without straying from your main idea. There is a saying that you should "always leave your audience wanting more." This reminder can be true for writers as well. Be sure that you include all of the points you wish to make; support them then with the detail and information that you have. When you have the form of your paper and its main points in mind, you are ready to write your outline.

THE FORMAL OUTLINE—WHAT IS IT?

A formal outline is a special format in which you display the details of your plan for writing your composition. It must follow an organized system of both numbers and letters to identify its various divisions and subdivisions.

You will begin your formal outline with a statement of your thesis. Then you will continue with an introduction, the main divisions and subdivisions of the presentation (which are called the body of the paper), and finally the paper's conclusion. The preparation of this outline requires a left margin of about an inch and a half. Top margins also may be an inch and a half. Each division and subdivision is indented five spaces from the left margin. The right margin must also be at least an inch to an inch and a half with the entire outline double-spaced, and an extra space between the subdivisions.

Roman numerals are used to indicate the main divisions of the topic about which you are writing. The capital letters A, B, C, etc. are at the next level of division or subdivision. Both the Roman numerals and the capital letters are indented. Then, as you follow subsubdivisions, additional supporting details are indicated by Arabic numerals such as 1, 2, 3, etc.

An important principle of the outline is that there is no division unless there are two or more parts. Therefore, if there is a Roman numeral I, there must be at least a Roman numeral II. If under the Roman numeral I there is subdivision, then there must be two parts, an A and a B:

    I – Subdivision
        A. Subdivision
        B. Subdivision

In other words, there is never a I without a II. There is never an A without a B, and so on down the line to the final subdivision. Conceivably, there can be Roman numerals I, II, and III without any further subdivisions, but this would indicate an outline and a paper that is missing important supporting details.

When you write your outline, be sure to keep all of the entries parallel. For example, you would group your ideas this way.

WRONG:

    A. Achieving good nutrition leads to good health
        1. Eating a good breakfast
        2. To include several servings of fruit

RIGHT:

    A. Achieving good nutrition leads to good health by
        1. *Eating* balanced meals
        2. *Including* several servings of fruits and vegetables

Notice how each subdivision has more than one entry and all of them are written in the same general tone. The headings do not overlap and the writing is parallel. Only the first word in each entry is capitalized, but all proper nouns (such as the name of a city) are capitalized. If you are writing a topic outline you do not use end punctuation. Sentence outlines require end punctuation just as though you are writing a regular sentence. It is *unnecessary* to caption the parts of outlines such as Thesis, Introduction, and so on. These words appear as guides in the following examples.

EXAMPLE OF TOPIC OUTLINE

(Title)
NAFTA: SECOND THOUGHTS FOR CANADA, MEXICO, AND THE U.S.

(Thesis Statement)
The North American Free Trade Agreement (NAFTA) has not proven to be a positive step toward economic stability for the countries involved.

(Introduction)
I. Effects of NAFTA
    A. Effects on Canada
    B. Effects on Mexico
    C. Effects on the United States

(Body)
II. Gains and losses for North American workers
    A. Gains and losses for Canada
        1. Decline of sales to U.S. markets
        2. Increased pollution
        3. Continued recession worsened by NAFTA
    B. Gains and losses for Mexico
        1. Relocation of U.S. industry to Mexican sites
        2. Pollution problems caused by new industry
        3. Decline of tourism
    C. Gains and losses for the United States
        1. Growth of high-tech jobs in U.S.
        2. Increased exports to Mexico
        3. Loss of industries to Mexico

(Conclusion)
III. Mexico, Canada, and the United States report that NAFTA has not lived up to its early expectations

EXAMPLE OF A SENTENCE OUTLINE

(Title)

NEW APPLICATIONS FOR AN OLD MEDICINE

(Thesis Statement)

Acupuncture, an ancient form of medical treatment associated with the Far East, is taking its place among the world's newest medical treatments.

(Introduction)

I. There is an interesting history associated with acupuncture.
    A. Its history goes back to ancient China.
    B. Very fine needles were used in Oriental medicine.
    C. Prejudices in Western countries prevented acupuncture's widespread use.

(Body)

II. Modern-day treatment uses electrical sources of stimulation.
    A. The use of acupuncture is now receiving modern-day research at well-known research centers.
    B. Its limitations and dangers are also being studied.

(Conclusion)

III. The protocol of modern-day acupuncture by accredited practitioners should be acknowledged and a fair examination of acupuncture's place in modern medicine should continue to be assessed.

CAPITALIZING IN OUTLINES

"To be or not to be: that is the question" was Hamlet's famous speech in Act III of Shakespeare's play by the same name; however, the student who is writing a paper could paraphrase this as, "To capitalize or not to capitalize, that is the question."

If you will note the example outlines on NAFTA and acupuncture in this chapter, you can see that the format and the use of capitals for either topic or sentence outline will appear something like this:

I. Main idea
   A. Subordinate idea
   B. Subordinate idea
      1. Example of subordinate idea
      2. Example of subordinate idea

AN ORGANIZATIONAL PLAN

Next you will need to choose an organizational plan. There are three ways to plan your outline and the writing of your paper as well. It may take some rearranging of your various groups of notes, but making these early decisions will reduce your problems with writing the paper later. *You also should check with your instructor when you choose your organizational plan.*

THREE ORGANIZATIONAL PLANS

There are several ways to arrange your paper. In some instances, one organizational plan is chosen, but a combination can be best:

1. Spatial order
2. Time order
3. Order of importance

Suppose you are writing a paper about Mexico's Cancun beaches. You may want to use a spatial order if this is to be a travel paper. You will need to describe where the beaches are located, their relationship to each other, the descriptive details of each beach, and the direction you take to visit the beaches. This is spatial ordering.

If you are writing about Cancun, Mexico, but you wish to make your point by following a visitor's activities throughout the day from morning until evening, you would use a time order or a time sequence. For example, you would probably begin with the early morning when you wake up. Your details are going to be descriptive, but your organization will take your reader with you from the time you wake in the morning to the time you go to bed at night. This is chronological ordering, or time ordering.

A paper such as the one on NAFTA best fits an order of importance. In this type of persuasive writing you wish to influence the reader and perhaps change his viewpoint. Begin with your strongest points and move from one point to the other to the supporting ideas. A strong conclusion will bring you back to this earlier idea.

CONSISTENCY IN OUTLINES

Many choices are offered a writer in preparing a formal outline. Most often, the instructor will tell you whether to prepare your outline as a topic outline or a sentence outline. If you are not instructed in this matter, you may need to consider the advantages of the two and then choose one that suits you best.

A topic outline is often easier to handle and more flexible. The sentence outline, however, will narrow down your ideas so that when you begin to write you will find it easier to follow. Never use both styles in the same outline.

EXAMPLE OF A POOR (INCONSISTENT) OUTLINE

I. Acupuncture has a long and ancient history going back to early Chinese medical practices.

    A. Early uses

    B. How the ancients did it

EXAMPLE OF A CONSISTENT SENTENCE OUTLINE

I. Acupuncture's history goes back to ancient China.

    A. Its early uses were varied.

    B. Ancient practitioners used needles at various points of the patient's body.

NOW YOU TRY IT!

EXERCISE 1: SHAPING AN OUTLINE

The following is a sentence outline. Change it to a topic outline on the lines provided below.

PANIC OVER FRUIT
by Marilyn Masters

Thesis Statement: The best action for the Food and Drug Administration to take in examining imported fruit is to destroy any shipments that might be contaminated with liquid-cyanide poisoning.

    I. Fruit such as grapes, peaches, blueberries, and plums are often treated with pesticides.

        A. Most countries that export these crops can be trusted to examine the fruit for the use of dangerous pesticides.

II. The United States maintains that it is difficult to test fruits for the dangerous liquid cyanide pesticides at borders.

    A. Careful restraints must be imposed on growers.

        1. Countries must develop reliable systems of inspection.

        2. They must act quickly.

    B. The best action that the United States can take is a final inspection at borders.

        1. Fruit must have a final inspection for pesticides.

        2. United States must use reliable inspections at borders.

    C. Fruit discovered to have been treated with liquid cyanide must be destroyed.

        1. Even if only two or three pieces of fruit are discovered, all of the fruit must be destroyed.

        2. Individual growers and the country of origin must bear the cost.

WRITE THE ABOVE OUTLINE WITH TOPICS INSTEAD OF SENTENCES:

_____

_____

_____

_____

_____

_____

_____

_____

_____

_____

(Responses will vary.)

COMPUTER-PRODUCED OUTLINES

Many computers now have word processing programs with a pre-defined outline format. This gives you several possible indentations, divisions, and subdivisions. Once you feel confident with these computer automatic outlining capabilities, you can edit, rewrite, and rearrange your outline as you progress with your paper. This will mean there is far less work for you to do when you have completed your research.

If your computer program does not include an outline capability, you can create one manually. The tabulator spacing is set at five spaces. This will give you several settings with which to experiment until you develop the outline you want to produce.

When you are typing your paper on a traditional or a word processing typewriter, you can still produce an effective and neat outline. The ability to do this depends on setting the tabs and using your machine's other features. In fact, a simple tab setting on a traditional machine will allow you to set up almost any format.

OUTLINE BEFORE YOU WRITE!

Even the most experienced writers find it hard to begin that final step to producing a good research paper—writing the paper itself. But having a well-prepared formal outline can be a great help through those early worries. Do not make the mistake of waiting until you have written your paper to outline it for the sake of meeting your requirements. One of the reasons for submitting an outline is to enable another person to follow the complexities of a paper. An outline also helps the instructor to anticipate the paper you will write. In fact, many instructors ask to see your outline early in the semester. This helps them to evaluate your ideas early enough to assist you. It also helps you to develop and maintain your research focus, and to organize your facts and ideas into an effective paper.

SUMMARY OF KEY POINTS IN THIS CHAPTER

Bibliographic notes and a working outline will provide a foundation for writing a formal outline.

1. A FORMAL OUTLINE FOLLOWS SPECIAL RULES.

- *Divisions and subdivisions are indicated through use of Roman numerals, alphabet, and Arabic numerals.*
- *There is never an A without a B; there is never a 1 without a 2; there is never an a) without a b).*
- *Topic outlines do not require complete sentences.*
- *Sentence outlines are prepared with complete sentences.*
- *The two are never mixed.*
- *Writing must be parallel.*

2. ORGANIZE RESEARCH NOTES.

- *Prepare a separate pile for each section.*
- *Use different color highlighter.*
- *Vary the color of ink for notes.*
- *Develop your own strategies.*

118

3. THERE ARE SEVERAL WAYS TO PREPARE A FORMAL OUTLINE.

■ *Type it on a traditional machine.*

■ *Prepare outline on a word processing typewriter.*

■ *Complete outline on personal computer with automatic outlining capabilities.*

4. COMPARE YOUR WRITING WITH YOUR OUTLINE TO KEEP YOUR PAPER CONSISTENT.

CHAPTER NINE

Documenting Your Research Paper

KEY VOCABULARY

(If you are unsure of meanings, check the glossary.)

Nouns	Verbs	Adjectives, Adverbs
citation	cite	complete
endnote	copyright	comprehensive
footnote	document	on-line
parenthesis	indent	portable
quotation	paraphrase	sparingly
summary		

DOCUMENTING YOUR RESEARCH

During a conversation with a friend, you often ask questions such as, "Where did you hear that?" or "Who said that?" It is only natural to want to know the source of the speaker's information. When you are writing a research paper, you are required to support and credit sources in much the same way. In other words, you document other writers' or speakers' words that are not your own original ideas so that your reader will know "who said that?" or "where did you read that?"

There are several methods that provide the documentation you will need as you prepare your research paper. However, not all of these are used at the same time in the same paper.

- Footnotes
- Endnotes
- Parenthetical documentation
- Paraphrase
- Quotations
- Summaries

WHEN TO CHOOSE A DOCUMENTATION STYLE

Before you begin your research you must decide whether the overall documentation style is going to be footnotes, endnotes, or parenthetical notes placed in the text itself. Therefore, when you write an index card, or when you download material from special computer-based sources, you should make your notes according to the style you or the instructor have chosen. However, certain information will always be included, such as the name of the material, its author, the publisher and location, page numbers, year published, a call number if it has one, and any electronic sources.

You should choose your documentation style as soon as you begin your research. You will need to know whether the overall documentation style is going to be footnotes or endnotes. For example, if you are using the MLA or APA documentation style, you must make this decision before you begin gathering your sources. Therefore, when you write an index card, or when you download material from a special computer-based source, you can make your notes accordingly.

WHEN TO INCLUDE YOUR NOTES IN YOUR TEXT

Deciding when to include your notes in the writing of your paper can be hard. Do you begin to add them as you write? Do you wait until you have written the first draft of your paper? Do you add them as you write? Do you only add citations as you are completing your manuscript?

The answer is that you include information all through the process of writing a research paper. In fact, making notes informally as you write your rough draft will help you to check information with your index cards at a later time.

STYLES OF CITATION

Many universities and colleges require numbered footnotes or endnotes for shorter research papers. The Modern Language Association (MLA) or the American Psychological Association (APA) usually require parenthetical citations for complex papers. Sometimes papers will use both but not within the same notation.

PARENTHETICAL DOCUMENTATION

Most schools recommend the MLA parenthetical method for citing sources in the humanities. This method does not disrupt the reading of the text. Instead of placing the necessary information about sources in a footnote or endnote, the writer will include within the text the author and page number on which the information appears in parentheses. At the end of the research paper, a page with a heading for *Works Cited* (MLA) or *References* (APA) lists the authors and complete information about the article, book, interview, etc. The APA style requires author, year, and page number. It is often used for social or natural sciences. The heading correctly used for APA is *References*. Only one style of parenthetical documentation is used in any one paper. (See Appendix.)

FOOTNOTES

A footnote is a numbered note of reference, explanation, or comment by the writer of a paper. Footnotes are consecutively numbered and are placed below the text, at the bottom of the manuscript page where it appears. The footnote indicates that the source of material is borrowed, and the information in the footnote tells where the writer found the material.

ENDNOTES

Endnotes are also numbered consecutively in the text of your paper. Then, at the end of your paper, you provide a list also numbered consecutively that includes all of the needed information on your sources. In other words, you do not include any notes on the page of the manuscript where the number appears. Instead, you are supplying your information at the end of your paper. Endnotes are often easier to prepare and will guide your reader to the correct information.

FOOTNOTE EXAMPLE

A footnote may be written in the following style. Notice in the example below that the author's name is first name, last name because footnotes are numbered sequentially and are not alphabetized.

Acupuncture's best-known use is for easing and relieving the pain of ailments such as arthritis, back problems, and rheumatism.[1]

---

[1]Barbara Nash, From Acupressure to Zen (Alameda, CA: Hunter House, Inc., 1996) 14.

With an endnote however, all that is necessary in the text is the number of the note typed one-half space above the material to be noted. In fact, the endnote is numbered consecutively like a footnote, following the material being noted.

When preparing the notation list at the end of your paper, use the word, notes, and center the title. The notes are then numbered just as they are numbered in the text and written in the basic format for footnotes.

Endnotes and footnotes contain the same information. The difference is that the note is numbered (just like a footnote) but it is not included below the text where it appears, but at the end with other reference matter. Also, endnotes are numbered consecutively and the author's name is first name, last name.

The final choice is whether to use more than one style of footnote or endnote as well as works cited or a reference page in the MLA or APA style. For most beginning research papers, one of the three styles is enough. It is usually best not to include endnotes if MLA Works Cited or the APA References are used in a particular paper.

When the footnote is too long to be completed on one page, it is continued on the following page. All of the information is begun on the page where the note first appears. The note for one book/one author is the basic format from which other notes or parenthetical references are written.

Most footnotes begin four lines (two double spaces) below the last line on the page. Footnotes are single-spaced, but if more than one footnote appears on a page, then double space between each individual note.

Word processing programs include instructions for preparing footnotes or endnotes. But if you are using a regular typewriter, you can mark each blank page with an erasable pencil mark before you begin to type.

Finally, there are many abbreviations that can be used in writing footnotes and endnotes. Some of the common ones are: ibid. (used for references previously cited in full) op. cit (in the work cited), loc. cit. (refers to the location of citation) vol. (volume), and pg. (page).

MLA OR APA PARENTHETICAL REFERENCES WITH FOOTNOTES OR ENDNOTES

Many universities and colleges recommend parenthetical reference methods such as MLA Works Cited style to be substituted for footnotes or endnotes; complex research papers may include both. The instructor will indicate whether to use footnotes, endnotes, and parenthetical citations or a combination.

Another style manual that is recommended for student papers, especially for theses and dissertations, is Kate L. Turabian's *A Manual for Writers of Term Papers, Theses, and Dissertation*. There are differences with Turabian, MLA, and APA, but all of them are used extensively in North American schools. However, the MLA, APA, or Turabian (University of Chicago styles) are never used in the same paper.

CITATION STYLES FOR ELECTRONIC SOURCES

Writing accurate citations for electronic sources such as a CD-ROM, the World Wide Web, or the media has always been difficult. Basing research papers on these sources was not encouraged in many classrooms. As a result, standards for writing correct and understandable citations for electronic material have been slow to develop.

Now, new guidelines have been established by Modern Language Association (MLA) in their second edition of *MLA Style*

Manual by Joseph Gibaldi. Herbert Lindenberger, Avalon Foundation Professor of Humanities at Stanford University and past president of MLA, added his foreword to the new edition. In this foreword, he offers a *uniform* set of guidelines.

So what are these electronic sources now beckoning even the most serious researchers? Here are a few of the more important ones that most college students will want to know.

- CD-ROMs
- Diskettes
- Magnetic tapes
- On-line books, periodicals, scholarly journals
- Reference databases
- Professional or personal sites
- Letters to the Editor on the Web
- Television or radio programs
- Sound recordings or sound chips
- Film or film clips
- Works of art on the Internet
- E-mail communication
- On-line maps, cartoons, advertisements
- WWW news articles or news services

DOCUMENTING ELECTRONIC SOURCES

Just as you may refer to another author's work to prepare your manuscript, your readers may want to build upon your research for *their* writing. Evaluating electronic sources and writing citations for these sources must be as accurate and helpful as possible—not always an easy task.

A lot of information on the Internet is self-published; therefore, you should rely on using authors or scholars who already have a reputation for accuracy and whose work is known to be both relevant and recent. The authenticity of the material makes the job of documenting it much simpler.

Still, finding the best way to document electronic sources is more challenging than referencing published material because the Web and TV and other media sources are not as organized as printed sources are. When the reliability of such material is difficult to establish, you can refer to the Uniform Resource Locator (URL) to check the network address. In using a network address, you should also include the access-mode identifier (*http*, *ftp*, *gopher*, *telnet*, *news*), and after the first single slash, any relevant path and file names.

<http://www.princeton.edu/-lancelot/>
(*MLA Style Manual*, page 210)

The *MLA Style Manual* also recommends using URLs in citing on-line works. Always use both printed and electronic sources for the same citation, if this is available.

Britannica Online. Vers, 97.1.1. Mar. 1997.
Encyclopedia Britannica. 29 Mar. 1997
<http:www.eb.com/.>

Many Internet publishers try to offer the same information that print sources do, but clear-cut organization does not yet exist. Some network addresses are used for such a short time that the address is no longer used by the time the paper is reviewed; therefore, combining both print and URL locations whenever possible gives a stability to a writer's citations. The following is an example of how the citation appears when both the printed and on-line sources are combined into one definitive citation:

Kotlowitz, Alex. The Other Side of the River. Nan A. Talese, Doubleday, 1998. <www.nanatelese.com> June 5, 1998.

TIPS FOR INCLUDING ELECTRONIC SOURCES

If anything, the new guidelines are meant to be helpful, not confusing. As you write your paper, keep the following tips in mind.

- Check sources for accuracy, point of view, quality, authority, and credibility.
- Follow the same documentation forms such as footnotes and endnotes that reflect sound writing styles.
- Use correct grammar in your citations for both.
- Resist overusing electronic jargon in citations.
- Include the dates of previous publications with electronic sources when such information is available.
- Supply more information for an electronic source than for a printed source.

Because these guidelines are designed mainly for the humanities, it is always a good idea to weigh the number of sources from printed origins and from electronic origins. A writer must be sure to complement the material from the Internet with the tried-and-true sources of printed matter that has withstood the test of time.

If you are writing a paper, you may want to consider this balance of reference sources: 20 percent electronic sources, 80 percent either printed sources or a combination of electronic and printed. Take the time to visit the stacks in your library, talk to a librarian, and come up with a sufficient number of printed sources to give your paper the balance and credibility it deserves.

WHAT MUST ALWAYS BE DOCUMENTED

The final check to decide whether a source must be documented is to ask, is this my own idea? If the answer is no, then the source must be documented.

Next, ask yourself if the material is from a published source or from TV, radio, or audio- or video-taped material. If the answer is yes, you must document. There is often confusion over whether material is copyrighted. This does not relate to documentation. The source must be acknowledged whether there is a copyright or not.

DOCUMENTING PRINT SOURCES

The following are examples of print sources that must be documented.

- A book with one or more authors
- A book with corporate authorship
- An edition other than the first
- A book in two or more volumes
- A reprint of an older work
- A translation of a book
- An essay or chapter from a book
- An essay or a chapter in a collection containing several authors' contributions compiled by an author
- Source information of periodicals
- An article in a scholarly journal
- An article in a periodical
- A signed article in a daily newspaper
- An unsigned article in a daily newspaper
- Encyclopedia articles
- Book reviews
- Interviews

MATERIAL NOT DOCUMENTED

You do not document well-known facts. For example, most readers know that Christopher Columbus discovered America in 1492. Therefore, you do not need to document such familiar information.

Moreover, excerpts commonly found in the Bible or in the classics do not need documentation. For example, "last but not least" is a quotation from Shakespeare, but it is so commonplace, it is considered cliché. It is best to avoid well-known sayings and facts. Try to find more interesting, unusual sources.

Writing that comes from you and you alone does not need to be documented. If for any reason you wish to clarify or expand your own writing, you might use a footnote, but not an endnote. Whenever possible, instructors will provide assistance along the way. Therefore, always consult with your instructor before making decisions about the way you have cited your research material.

(The following styles of citations can be useful for most research papers.)

BOOKS WITH ONE AUTHOR

MLA   Davies, Robertson. <u>What's Bred in the Bone</u>. Markham, Ontario, Canada: Penguin, 1986.

APA   Davies, R. (1986). <u>What's bred in the bone</u>. Markham, Ontario, Canada: Penguin.

BOOKS WITH MORE THAN ONE AUTHOR

MLA   Matthews, Candace, and Joanne Marino. <u>Professional Interactions: Oral Communication Skills in Science, Technology, and Medicine</u>. Englewood Cliffs, New Jersey: Prentice Hall Regents, 1990.

APA   Matthews, C. & Marino, J. (1990). <u>Professional interactions: oral communication skills in science, technology, and medicine</u>. Englewood Cliffs, NJ: Prentice Hall Regents.

131

PAMPHLETS, BROCHURES WITH NO AUTHOR NAMED

MLA   Microref: WordPerfect for Windows. Version 5.2, Northbrook, IL, 1993.

APA   Microref: WordPerfect for windows. (1993). Version 5.2, Northbrook, IL.

ENTRY IN ENCYCLOPEDIA

MLA   The Encyclopedia of World Biography. Vol. 4, pgs 134-136. McGraw Hill Book Co., New York: 1993.

APA   The encyclopedia of world biography. (1993). Vol. 4, pgs 134-136. New York, NY: The McGraw Hill Book Co.

TRANSLATION

MLA   Esquivel, Laura. Like Water for Chocolate: A Novel in Monthly Installments, with Recipes, Romances, and Home Remedies. Trans. Carol Christensen and Thomas Christensen. New York: Knopf, 1976.

APA   Esquivel, L. (1976). Like water for chocolate: a novel in monthly installments, with recipes, romances, and home remedies. (Trans. C. Christensen and T. Christensen.) New York, NY: Knopf.

ARTICLE IN NEWSPAPER OR MAGAZINE

MLA   "New Research Links Gene to Most Breast Tumors." The Washington Post Friday, 3 Nov. 1995: A 3.

APA   New research links gene to most breast tumors. (1995, Nov. 3). The Washington Post A 3.

CD-ROMS AND OTHER PORTABLE SOFTWARE

MLA   The Oxford English Dictionary. 2nd ed. CD-ROM. New York: Oxford University Press, 1992.

ON-LINE SOURCES OR INFORMATION FROM E-MAIL

MLA   <u>Tips on Cooking Turkey</u>. World Wide Web (service provider).

<http://www.butterball.com.>

A REVIEW

Shreve, Anita. <u>The Weight of Water</u>. Back Bay Books, Little Brown & Company, Boston: Reading Group Guide Review. <http//www.littlebrown.com>

NOTES FROM FILMS AND VIDEOS

MLA   <u>The Jewel in the Crown</u>. Paul Scott. Actress, Peggy Ashcroft. Masterpiece Theater. WETA, Washington, DC.

PUNCTUATION FOR CITATIONS

Punctuation differs with various styles of citation. However, just as there is a basic form of citation that is reasonably consistent among the authorities, there is also a style of punctuation that is basic to writing documentation for research papers.

PUNCTUATION EXAMPLE

Way, Brian. <u>Development through Drama</u>. London, England: Longman Group Limited, 1973.

(handwritten annotations: last name, comma, first name, period, single space, underlined title, period, city, comma, country, colon, publisher, comma, date, period)

QUOTATIONS

Quotations, that is the use of a speaker's or writer's direct words, can add interest to your research paper. Short quotations, under thirty or forty words, can be used directly in the text of the paper.

However, longer quotations are set off within the paper by spacing. When the material is indented, it is not necessary to include quotation marks.

When a quotation is longer, it may be indented such as these exact words quoted from *Alternative Healing* by Mark Kastner and Hugh Burroughs (page 50):

> In Sanskrit, the ancient language of India, *Charkas* means "what revolves" or "wheel," indicating that these force centers are wheels of energy. According to traditional yoga philosophy, the charkas are subtle force centers that vitalize and control the physical body.

The writer also has the choice of paraphrasing excerpts from other books or articles. The source still should be documented, however, even if the information is in your own words.

For example, a student writer might paraphrase a description of a small town in Canada in a research paper about Robertson Davies' book, *What's Bred in the Bone*. The student need not use the exact words from the book but could write the description in a paraphrase.

The following quotation is directly from Robertson Davies' novel, "To begin, when Francis was born there, Blairlogie was not the Jumping-off Place, and would have strongly resented any such suggestion. It thought of itself as a thriving town, and for its inhabitants, the navel of the universe."

A paraphrase of this:

> In Robertson Davies' book, *What's Bred in the Bone*, his character Francis was born in Blairlogie where its inhabitants would never regard his birth as their only distinction.

Notice that a paraphrase does not require quotation marks, but the source of the general idea must be documented. That is, the author and the title of the book, article, or special piece should refer to the source of the material.

SUMMARIES

Summaries are condensations of several pages or chapters or the entire book or article. Summaries should only be a few sentences in length. The importance of a summary is that it gives the student an opportunity to briefly discuss a book or article in a paper without plagiarizing.

The summary must include a reference to its source. It must be accurate and should not include your own ideas.

To summarize the several headings of this chapter, we might write the following.

- Keep correct information on bibliographic cards and also make short preliminary notes within the text as you write your first drafts.
- Document the sources within your text through a footnote, an endnote, a direct quotation as directed by the MLA style system, or the APA method.
- Insert your quotation, paraphrases, or summaries properly.

DOCUMENTATION CHECKUP

- Are footnotes placed correctly?
- Are essential sources documented?
- Are acronyms and periodical names given once in full?
- Have names been spelled consistently in notes?
- Is punctuation consistent? Is capitalization consistent?
- Have you included network addresses, dates researched?

SUMMARY OF KEY POINTS IN THIS CHAPTER

When you write a research paper, you are asked to support and credit your ideas.

1. **THERE ARE SEVERAL WAYS TO TELL YOUR READERS WHERE YOU GOT YOUR INFORMATION AND TO WHOM YOU ARE CREDITING THE INFORMATION**

   ■ *Footnotes*

   ■ *Endnotes*

   ■ *Parenthetical references with Works Cited or References at the end of the manuscript*

   ■ *Paraphrase*

   ■ *Direct quotation*

2. **WHAT MUST BE CITED**

   ■ *Information, ideas, and statistics and their sources such as surveys, etc., conducted by someone else*

   ■ *Lines from a poem*

   ■ *Lines from a novel or a nonfiction book*

   ■ *Quotation from a short story*

   ■ *Interviews*

   ■ *Videos*

   ■ *Audios*

   ■ *Movies*

   ■ *Stage plays*

   ■ *Electronic sources and data accessed*

3. **EVEN IF COPYRIGHTS HAVE EXPIRED, IT IS AN ACADEMIC REQUIREMENT TO GIVE THE SOURCE OF THE MATERIAL. FOR EXAMPLE, A WRITER MIGHT WANT TO QUOTE FROM PLATO'S <u>REPUBLIC</u>. EVEN THOUGH IT IS IN THE PUBLIC DOMAIN (NOT COPYRIGHTED), EXCERPTS MUST BE CITED.**

4. **MATERIAL THAT DOES NOT REQUIRE DOCUMENTATION CAN BE SOURCES THAT ARE FAMILIAR, SUCH AS QUOTATIONS FROM THE BIBLE OR FACTS WHOSE ORIGINS ARE KNOWN.**

CHAPTER TEN

Revising and Editing Your Paper

KEY VOCABULARY

(If you are unsure of meanings, check the glossary.)

Nouns	Verbs	Adjectives, Adverbs
acronym	eliminate	blemished
checklist	omit	clearly
development	revise	coherent
errors	state	consistent
examples		effectively
fragments		fused
homonym		relevant
restatement		supportive
unity		

REVISING YOUR PAPER

When you are cooking a special dish, the final step is to taste it. You check it for flavor, spiciness, and consistent quality. Finally, you serve it to your family and guests. Revising a research paper is like preparing special food. This final step does not mean that you will make a lot of major changes in your paper, but you can revise and improve it without losing its original continuity and organization.

What's more, your research paper will be evaluated on how effectively you have communicated your ideas. To make certain that you have accomplished what you set out to write also depends on how successfully you revise and edit your paper. Correcting the grammar, punctuation, and spelling of your paper needs special attention. Revising involves checking your ideas and the accuracy of your paper; editing examines the mechanical aspects of your paper such as grammar, punctuation, and spelling.

GRADE YOUR PAPER YOURSELF

One way to begin the revision process is to grade your paper yourself. For a short time, pretend that <u>you</u> are the professor and the paper is one you have never seen before. As you read it, decide upon one of the following grades.

A–Outstanding
B–Very good
C–Average
D–Passing

Now, do not take off your imaginary teacher's hat. Read your paper critically. Would you give this paper an A, B, or C? Worse yet, would you say that it is barely passing?

COHERENCE, UNITY, AND CLARITY

As you look at your paper, it is very unlikely that you will give yourself an A. Until a paper goes through the revision process, it is not really polished enough to receive the highest grade. So what can you do to make this B or C paper into an A paper? First, look at the paper from beginning to end. Read it for coherence, unity, and clarity. Does one idea lead to the next idea smoothly? Have you organized and written according to your outline? Make certain you have a clearly stated introduction. Go over the body of the paper to be sure it supports and explains your thesis. Finally, reread the conclusion. Is it strong? Does it restate the original premise of the paper? Does it bring your paper to a satisfying conclusion?

RULES FOR REVISION

Here are some rules to follow as you continue your revision of your paper.

1. State and stay on your research focus.
2. Keep your ideas organized.
3. Include enough details to support your statements.
4. Vary the length of sentences.
5. Choose effective words.
6. End with a restatement of your thesis.

Review your paper to see that it states and stays with the research focus. (Do not depend on the title of the paper to do this.) At the same time you want to capture your reader's interest. Ask yourself if you have used precise, interesting words.

THE BODY

As you begin to examine the body of your paper, you want to include supporting examples to strengthen your main ideas. If you have not, you can expand this part of your paper without making more changes.

Also, you can check once more to be sure that your details and supporting material are relevant to your main ideas. When you prepared your outline, certain details may have seemed appropriate. Now that you have written the paper, you may decide they are not. Removing extra material is accomplished best during revision.

This final step also can reveal passages that are confusing. Consider rearranging your supportive material if it does not fit. By placing an example in another paragraph, you may clear up a troublesome part of the writing.

THE CONCLUSION

As you continue to revise your paper, consider its conclusion. As a writer you should provide your reader with a satisfactory closure. You do not want to stop writing without restating the main points of your paper.

Finally, never introduce new ideas in your conclusion. The ending of the paper must only reiterate the main thesis of your paper in an interesting and different way. Try to avoid writing, "in conclusion," but give the feeling of a conclusion by the basic sense of your last paragraph.

In different words, and with renewed emphasis, you must now bring your reader back to the beginning of the paper before you bring it to closure. It is often effective to briefly summarize your paper in the last paragraph. Remember, these are your final words. Therefore, keep your conclusion short, never introduce new ideas, and leave your reader satisfied.

VARIETY IN SENTENCES

Imagine that you are the reader of your paper, not the writer. Try analyzing it from the reader's point of view. If you begin to find that your writing becomes monotonous, repetitious, or hard to follow, you may be having problems with your sentence construction.

1. SIMPLE SENTENCE

Contains a subject, predicate, and additional information in the form of prepositional phrases or other means.
Example: The white van speeded through the intersection.

2. COMPOUND SENTENCE

Has two or more independent clauses that are related.
Example: Butterflies appear fragile, but they are capable of traveling hundreds of miles.

3. COMPLEX SENTENCE

Has one independent clause and one subordinate clause.
Example: When you are planning a trip (subordinate clause), you should telephone more than one airline to compare prices.

4. COMPOUND/COMPLEX SENTENCE

Combines both compound sentence and complex sentence:
Example: The storm destroyed the pine trees (independent clause), which we planted in the driveway, (subordinate clause) but it did not harm the red maples near the house (independent clause).

Other ways to vary your writing is to use different types of sentence construction. The four following types of sentences can give you different structures and emphasize various ideas.

DECLARATIVE

Example: The white truck was speeding dangerously through the intersection.

INTERROGATIVE

Example: Was the white truck speeding dangerously when it entered the intersection?

IMPERATIVE

Example: Write down the license number of that white truck.

EXCLAMATORY

Example: Call the police! That white truck is speeding dangerously!

CUT AND PASTE

Now that you have decided on your revisions, do you know how to make them? If you are working on a traditional typewriter, you can cut and paste. This method requires a pair of scissors and a roll of cellophane tape.

For example, when you decide to move certain copy, first cut it from a photocopy (never from the original) and paste it to the text where you will include it in the final typing. The total effect can be neatly put back together, and you can then photocopy the final results. However, the paper itself will have to be retyped.

Word processing programs for a computer also have a cut and paste feature. In this, you can mark the copy you want to change to another part of your paper, click on the cut portion, move the marker to the alternative placement, and then click on paste and save your changes.

Does cutting and pasting happen often? The answer here is yes, more often than many writers might like to admit. Primarily, research and writing any paper is a creative process. Creative processes sometimes call for changes, even at the last minute. Creativity also demands a lot of trial and error—that is, making an attempt to improve a work, and then, discovering that the original is best after all.

THE FINAL CHECK

The previous steps in reviewing your paper are called substantive editing. Now you are ready to go on with the mechanical editing—that is, the checking for grammar usage, misspelled words, agreement with verb forms, word choices, verb tenses, sentence structure, capitalization, and punctuation.

An editorial checklist is helpful to writers who are giving their papers a final revision and editing.

Here is a list of common writing errors. The error is followed by a correct example.

RUN-ON SENTENCE

A big city's best restaurants are usually expensive you have to consult a guide book to find good food at a reasonable price.
Correction: A big city's best restaurants are usually expensive. You have to consult a guide book to find good food at a reasonable price.

INCOMPLETE SENTENCE

Want to go to a restaurant with a pleasant atmosphere?
Complete sentence: Do you want to go to a restaurant with a pleasant atmosphere?

INCORRECT CAPITALIZATION

She has always wanted to visit france.
Correction: She has always wanted to visit France.
(Refer to your dictionary for correct capitalization. Do not rely on memory.)

MISSING PUNCTUATION

I want to order an appetizer entrée and a salad.
Correction: I want to order an appetizer, an entrée, and a salad.

WRITE OUT SYMBOLS

More than 50% of the class did not pass.
Correction: More than 50 percent of the class did not pass.

SPELL OUT NUMBERS ONE THROUGH NINE (OR NINETY)

Any 2 of the examples will be enough.
Correction: Any two of the examples will be enough.

INCORRECT WORD ORDER
He three times made the trip to Italy.
Correction: He made the trip to Italy three times.

MEANING NOT CLEAR
Give her a ring.
Correction: Give her a phone call.

POOR WORD CHOICE
Patrick was on Chicago on a business trip.
Correction: Patrick was in Chicago on a business trip.

INCORRECT VERB TENSE
She is working here since February.
Correction: She has been working here since February.

INCORRECT SUBJECT/VERB AGREEMENT IN PRESENT TENSE
They has two daughters.
Correction: They have two daughters.

INCORRECT WORD FORMS
This is more easier.
Correction: This is easier.

UNNECESSARY WORDS
The students entered into the classroom.
Correction: The students entered the classroom.

MISSING WORDS
Tourists docks to see the fishermen's catch.
Correction: Tourists gather at the docks to see the fishermen's catch.

LACK OF PARALLEL CONSTRUCTION
The movie was about to be good, bad, and ugly.
Correction: It was a case of the good, the bad, and the ugly.

RULES FOR CAPITALIZATION

The choice of what to capitalize and what not to capitalize is a difficult decision all writers must make. Many institutions provide their own recommendations in a special style sheet, but if you are on your own, you can follow a few simple rules.

BE CONSISTENT

Whatever your choice of capitalization, the most important consideration is to be consistent. If you capitalize the title Superintendent as a part of a proper noun in one sentence and leave the word without a capital in another, you create a problem for your reader. Difficult capitalization decisions should be made with the help of a reliable dictionary or style book.

These are some examples of what you must capitalize.

- ### THE FIRST WORD IN A SENTENCE
  The baseball season opened last week.

- ### PROPER NOUNS SUCH AS NAMES OF PEOPLE
  Marilyn Monroe was an American movie star.

- ### NATIONALITIES, RACES, AND LANGUAGES
  Many nations in Africa speak French as an official language.

- ### NAMES, TITLES, AND QUOTATIONS ARE CAPITALIZED EXACTLY THE SAME IN BOTH THE ORIGINAL LANGUAGE AND THE TRANSLATION
  The name of the movie was based upon the Latin quotation "Quo vadis."

- ### DAYS OF THE WEEK, THE MONTHS, AND SOMETIMES THE SEASONS ARE CAPITALIZED
  Some companies permit employees to dress casually on Fridays. On Mondays, Tuesdays, Wednesdays, and Thursdays employees must wear more formal attire.

■ NAMES OF PUBLIC PLACES AND OTHER MAN-MADE STRUCTURES

Bridges—Golden Gate Bridge

Expressways—Brooklyn-Queens Expressway

Space Stations—Mir

Spacecraft—*Apollo 13*

Ships—The *Bismarck*

Towers—Eiffel Tower

Tombs—Tomb of the Unknown Soldier

Museums—British Museum

Trains—Orient Express

■ PERSONAL AND PROFESSIONAL TITLES

Prime Minister Churchill was an outstanding communicator.

■ NAMES OF DEITY IN DIFFERENT RELIGIONS

Christ, Allah, Brahma, the Holy Ghost

■ NAMES OF RELIGIONS

Buddhism, Catholicism, Judaism

■ PARKS, CITIES, STATES, COUNTIES, AND OTHER DERIVATIVES OF SPECIAL NAMES

Hyde Park is in London, England.

■ THE FIRST LETTER OF THE FIRST WORD WITHIN A QUOTATION

The Washington Post reports, "In certain parts of rural Texas, motorists have a new traffic hazard to dodge: emus on the loose."

■ THE PRONOUN *I* BUT NOT OTHER PRONOUNS UNLESS THEY START A SENTENCE

I have an idea! She can send her report directly to the company.

■ **NAMES AND ABBREVIATIONS OF ORGANIZATIONS AND INSTITUTIONS**

The World Health Organization, a part of the United Nations, is respected in most countries.

■ **WORDS IN TITLES, EXCEPT FOR PREPOSITIONS, ARTICLES (UNLESS IT BEGINS THE TITLE), AND OTHER SHORT WORDS**

Laura Esquival's book, *Like Water for Chocolate*, was translated from Spanish to English.

WHAT NOT TO CAPITALIZE

Frequently used expressions are not capitalized, even if they are proper nouns; for example, you do not capitalize the name of a country when it is a commonly used adjective.

We ordered french fries with our luncheon because they were included as part of a special price.

HEADLINE-STYLE CAPITALIZATION

The place for headline-style capitalization is for heads, or sub-heads, and, as the name implies, for newspaper and magazine titles. Do not use headline capitals to cover up capitalization problems you are not sure of. When you put THE NEW YORK TIMES in headline caps, you are demonstrating to your instructor that you did not check the proper capitalization for newspaper titles.

NEVER CAPITALIZE COMMON NOUNS

Another rule that is important for speakers of other languages is this: Do not capitalize common nouns such as school, church, office, restaurant. The confusion arises for those writers who are used to capitalizing nouns and other parts of speech in their first language. There is more confusion because these same common nouns *are* capitalized when they are part of a title, an official citation, and several other such designations.

GUIDE TO SPELLING IN ENGLISH

English words are related in most cases to a particular family of spelling systems; that is, many English words have different origins. The "ph" spellings come from the Greek word for "sound," and words ending in *tien* have French origins. Latin, German, Anglo-Saxon, Spanish, Portuguese, and even Finnish words have been absorbed into the English language. Often the spelling is different, as is the pronunciation.

English words tend to carry special information in smaller units. An example of this is our extensive use of prefixes and suffixes. *Pre* is a prefix. It can be used as part of the words *preschool, prepare,* or *premonition.* While each word is quite different in meaning, its prefix *pre* means to come before.

The more we know about the English language, the better spellers we will become, which is why many early learners of English have a difficult time with written work. As they advance with their spoken language, however, their written language also improves without studying specific words.

Several strategies can help the nonnative speaker to write with more accuracy.

- ✔ Always examine the word within context.
- ✔ Determine the pattern of the word and relate it to a group of other words.
- ✔ Analyze the vowel sounds. Certain groups of words have the same sound and consequently the same spelling; for example, the long E sound for words such as relieve, conceive, or receipt.

✔ Always check your pronunciation. We tend to spell as we pronounce; therefore, incorrect sounds will produce incorrect spelling. If we say "liberry" for library, we will probably misspell the word.

✔ Try different associations to other words to learn their spellings. They do not have to be sensible, but are just memory aids. An example of this is the spelling for the head of a high school. It should be "principal" and in order to spell this correctly we might think, "The principal is a *pal* to his students." You then remember to not confuse the word with the other similar word, principle.

✔ Carefully study the prefixes and suffixes. This strategy can help you to spell hundreds of words. It also can help with comprehension. A few of the most common are: *mis* (as in misspelled) and *un* as in unreal. *Pre* is easy to remember and is involved in dozens of familiar words such as *pre*liminary, *pre*lude, and *pre*mature.

✔ When words end in hard consonants such as b, p, and t, the letter is doubled, as in hotter and stabbed.

✔ In words ending in *y*, do not forget to change the letter to *i* as in reality—realities.

English has so many irregularities and exceptions, that it takes years to become an accurate speller. Always take the time to check words either in the dictionary or on the computer's spell checker. You may still have to make certain decisions as to how you will spell a word in a particular paper. If this is the case, the final caution is the same as with capitalization: Be consistent.

AVOID AWKWARDLY PLACED MODIFIERS

Another suggestion not associated with spelling, but just as important, is to check for words that are placed so that they are hard to understand or may lead to ambiguities. The most obvious misplaced modifiers are sometimes a source of great amusement in a classroom. No writer should ever say, "Oh, you know what I meant." We readers usually do not.

An example of misplaced modifiers:

The man and woman falsely accused of forgery would happily never again live there.

Note the placement of *happily*. Does the writer mean that it is a good thing that the couple will never again live there? More likely, the writer means that they can never live happily at that location following their false accusation.

DANGLING MODIFIERS

During the revision process, you must search for dangling modifiers. Because the modifier that dangles is one that is often implied rather than directly stated, it can elude even the most determined editing. The writer knows the meaning, but the reader will have a hard time understanding the sentence or paragraph. An example of this is in the following sentence.

Riding a bicycle to work, the benefits surprised us.

Such a sentence can confuse the reader. Who is riding the bicycle? Here is a better sentence.

We rode a bicycle to work for a week and were surprised at the benefits.

READ BACKWARDS

It is also helpful when you are checking your paper for grammar and spelling errors to read your paper one sentence at a time—and to read it from the end to the beginning. As strange as this sounds, working back to the beginning of the paper keeps you focused on the task of looking for errors and does not permit you to think of the content of the paper.

OTHER EDITING TIPS

Proofread your final draft at least twice. It is best to wait several hours, or overnight, before you read it the second time. Also, this is a good time to photocopy your paper. Never submit a paper without keeping a photocopy for your records. Then, should something happen to the paper, you have your own copy to prove that you did your work and it was submitted on time.

The memory of spell check programs includes thousands of words. They are a tremendous help in finding typographical errors and will correct them in one or two keystrokes.

However, you must read the work carefully before deciding upon certain spellings because the word may be a homonym. It can appear either correct or incorrect in your text, when actually, you have a particular use in mind for which the computer cannot discriminate. An example of this is the sound-alike words such as *their, there,* and *they're.* The spell check will not find your mistake as a spelling mistake. Keep in mind, though, that a mistake with one of these words could easily be detected through an efficient and intuitive grammar check.

Also, proper nouns or special words not listed in the spell check will be a problem. For example, acronyms, such as MLA for

Modern Language Association, will appear on the screen as misspelled. The way to avoid this is to add that term or letters to the spell check list.

An example of this could be through the software on a computer. These programs search your research paper electronically against grammar usage, punctuation rules, and other problems such as overuse of the passive voice. There are style checks that include that very sensitive subject of gender bias. As an example of how these help, if the grammar check warns you that you have used the word *greedy* many times in a paragraph, several synonyms are suggested. For example, *covetous* is a good choice to replace *greedy*.

QUESTIONS

1. Do I have an important idea to communicate to my reader?
2. Do my title and introduction catch the reader's attention?
3. Does my first paragraph convey the main idea (thesis) in an interesting way?
4. Does each paragraph in the body of the paper have coherence, unity, and clear development?
5. Have I developed the body of my paper according to the importance of ideas? If not, have I used a chronological or spatial order?
6. Do I lead my reader smoothly from one paragraph to another?
7. Do I begin my paragraphs with a topic sentence?
8. Do I fill my paragraphs with significant details?
9. Do I refrain from overemphasizing, writing down, or preaching to the reader?
10. Do I employ interesting words without overdoing the multisyllable ones to impress my reader?

Finally, you should ask yourself, am I satisfied with the way I have organized and arranged my research paper? Have I given my paper a clear thesis and proper support? Have I checked my list for good grammar usage? Have I made certain I have not misspelled words, have not used abbreviations incorrectly, and have avoided unnecessary punctuation, markings, and directions?

Now that you have reviewed your research paper, revised it, corrected it, and made extra copies, you can ask yourself these final questions—is it my best effort? Can I be proud of my work? If the answer is yes, you have completed your research paper!

SUMMARY OF KEY POINTS IN THIS CHAPTER

1. ACHIEVING COHERENCE, UNITY, AND CLARITY

2. VARYING THE CONSTRUCTION OF YOUR SENTENCES
- *Simple sentences*
- *Compound sentences*
- *Complex sentences*
- *Compound/complex sentences*

3. CUT-AND-PASTE TECHNIQUES WITH A TRADITIONAL TYPEWRITER REQUIRE ONLY A PAIR OF SCISSORS AND CELLOPHANE TAPE. IT IS A QUICK WAY TO REVISE AND REARRANGE WORK DONE ON A CONVENTIONAL MACHINE.

4. MAKING YOUR FINAL CHECK
- *Read it backwards.*
- *Refer to a good list of checks for the final review.*

APPENDICES

Sample Essay

Edward Weeks, the ninth editor of Atlantic Magazine, *wrote a foreward for Little, Brown, and Company's 1938 edition of* A Dictionary of English Synonyms and Synonymous Expressions *by Richard Soule. The foreword was written in the form of a short essay consisting of several paragraphs: the introduction, which states what the essay is about, and supporting paragraphs that clarify and expand the essay's original premise. Mr. Week's final paragraph brings the essay to a humorous and satisfying conclusion.*

FOREWORD

The only man I have known who made an actual, not theoretical, choice of the three books he would want on a desert island was James Norman Hall. In 1932, when Jim and his close friend and collaborator Charlie Nordhoff were writing their great trilogy, *Mutiny on the Bounty*, it became necessary for one of them to visit Pitcairn Island, where the mutineers had hidden themselves and where their descendants still live. Pitcairn, a tiny shark's tooth of an island, rises out of the Pacific twelve hundred miles distant from Tahiti, where the authors were at work. Jim decided to make the voyage on a two-masted, ninety-ton trading schooner, and knowing that he would have many days at sea, he took with him Borrow's *The Bible in Spain*, Wordsworth's poems, and a single volume of his new set of the *Encyclopedia of Britannica*—the volume covering from MED to MUM.

Words are of course the tools of a writer, and while Hall was sopping up all this curious information he was also storing away fresh, keen-edged words, like new finds in the storeroom of his vocabulary. Dictionaries are an indispensable part of every author's workshop, and equally so for editors, who have to check and sometimes query their contributors' English.

Later, in 1938, I became the ninth editor of *The Atlantic* and moved into the big front office at 8 Arlington St. (Boston). I found awaiting me on the Directors' table a small clutch of source books; they included Soule's *Dictionary of English Synonyms*.

A book like Soule's *Synonyms* is habit forming. You go in search of a word or a figure of speech which will better express what you have in mind, and having found it, you linger on the page to absorb others. Suppose we take the area which Jim Hall found so engrossing, from MED to MUM. I have just used the word *meditate* in a piece I am writing.

Now I want to revert to the same thought in the more lively way. I look up *meditate*. I find: *contemplate, study, chew, ruminate, revolve in mind, ponder, cogitate, cudgel one's brains, collect one's thoughts, advise with one's pillow*—I have never heard that one before. It makes me smile and will make others too. So I jot it down.

But now that I am in the word-shop, I begin to sample others. *Mellow—soft, rich, delicate, tipsy, fuddled, high seas over. . .mendacious—lying, deceitful. . .minx—hussy, jade, baggage, pert girl. . .*and so on, drifting down to *Mum—silent, mute, speechless, dumb*. But who wants to be mum?

Edward Weeks
Soule's Dictionary
of English Synonyms

Sample Research Papers— Two Styles

The two research papers that follow illustrate two styles of documentation: one is based upon the MLA parenthetical style and the other uses endnotes.

In your academic paper will need one of the three following styles of listed sources: Bibliography; Works Cited (MLA); and References (APA).

When your instructor requires a list of sources, you will need to choose one of these. All three formats are similar. For example, the most basic form is for a bibliography. This is used with footnotes or endnotes. For the APA or MLA form of documentation, you will want to use the same format with the few variations indicated in Chapter Nine for Documentation.

Most bibliography formats give all sources, even those that are not necessarily referred to in the manuscript. Some instructors may call this a working bibliography.

In the MLA format, you have two options. You may list your sources at the end of the paper and list all sources consulted. Or you may list only those sources referred to in the paper. This is the format that will be entitled *Works Cited* and will appear at the end of your paper. The APA lists of sources is referred to as *References*.

Please note that the title page and sentence outline may be used with both papers. Remember to check with your instructor for final guidelines.

New Applications for an Ancient Medicine

By
Emma Perry

English Composition 206
Professor John Smith
Date

(SENTENCE OUTLINE)

NEW APPLICATIONS FOR AN ANCIENT MEDICINE

(Thesis Statement)
Acupuncture is an ancient Oriental medicine that is being studied
for its effectiveness as an alternative medicine.

I. There is a history of thousands of years of the practice of
acupuncture in the Far East.
   A. Written records on acupuncture date back to 2800 B.C.
   B. Prejudices in Western countries prevented its acceptance.

II. Because patients feared the use of needles, acupuncture was
not accepted in other parts the world.

III. Acupuncture is a vital part of today's medical practice in
China and other Asian countries.
   A. Accredited acupuncturists focus on preventive medicine.
   B. Acupuncture is also a vital part of modern surgery in
   Asian countries.
      1. Thyroidectomy and prostate operations are
      examples of successful anesthetic applications.
      2. Acupuncture is not always as successful in
      abodominal operations. Surgeons may use mod-
      ern anesthetic techniques.

IV. Modern-day treatments often include electrical sources of
stimulation rather than needles.
   A. Extensive studies in the United States and Europe
   have helped dispel old prejudices.

B. Research is underway at well-known medical facilities such as the National Institutes of Health in Bethesda, Maryland.

V. Acupuncture in Western countries is a combination of therapies.

VI. Many physicians refer their patients to accredited acupuncturists for certain chronic diseases.
  A. Patients with lower back pain that has not improved with traditional medicine are referred to acupuncturists.
  B. Sufferers of migraine headaches report improvement after referral to acupuncture specialists.

VII. Acupuncture also treats certain diseases that are affected by stress.
  A. Some stomach ulcer patients report improvement.
  B. Psoriasis sufferers report fewer problems.

VIII. Problems in the United States and other North American countries have arisen with the growth of acupuncturists who lack knowledge and skill.
  A. As a result of poor practictioners, acupuncture has gotten a bad reputation.
  B. In some areas, accreditation of acupuncturists is either very poor or completely lacking.
  C. Practitioners can vary greatly and sometimes pose a threat to a patient's health.
  D. Patients who search for this method of therapy are warned against the fakes in the business.

IX. As a whole, acupuncture is slowly gaining recognition. Research is taking place throughout the world at well-known centers such as the National Institutes of Health. It will be many years before acupuncture is fully accepted and controlled in the West, but there is every indication that there are many applications for an old medicine in Western countries.

(USING MLA PARENTHETICAL CITATIONS)

NEW APPLICATIONS FOR AN ANCIENT MEDICINE

Acupuncture is a part of traditional Oriental medicine that is now being studied for its effectiveness as an alternative or adjuvant medical treatment in Western countries as well. With more open communication between China and the United States, and other Western European nations, a sharing of medical knowledge has also taken place. Consequently there is a new interest and acknowledgment of some of the successes of acupuncture treatment. In fact, it could be said that since the 1970s, there has been an increase in the interest in acupuncture with many new applications for an old medicine.

Its name, *acupuncture*, means to prick with a needle. "It is the art of expertly and painlessly piercing the skin with disposable needles at different points," writes Barbara Nash. What's more, acupuncture, which originated in China, has a history that can be traced back approximately 5,000 years (Nash 12).

However, in the eighteenth and nineteenth centuries, Western patients did not trust the use of needles. This common practice involves using needles for stimulation of the Ho Ku points, which in turn causes Teh-ch'i—a tingling sensation that often seems to relieve pain at distant points of the body (Collinge 21). This prejudice is said to have prevented the serious study of acupuncture in Western countries. Still, an interest lived on among a handful of medical practitioners. In fact, after years of debate on acupuncture methodology, there are currently several serious efforts to evaluate acupuncture's effectiveness in diagnosing illness, treating illness, managing chronic disorders, relieving pain, and promoting health through prevention and maintenance (Kastner, Burroughs 3).

In the United States, acupuncture is receiving special attention as an alternative or adjuvant treatment for many diseases, especially those that are related to the central nervous system or to stress-induced illnesses. But acupuncture remains a vital part of medical practice in contemporary China and other Asian countries. In fact, acupuncture has been the major type of medical treatment there and was only recently integrated with Western medical techniques beginning with nineteenth-century missionaries. However, one of the most dramatic reports of the successful use of acupuncture during a surgical procedure came from James Reston, who accompanied President Nixon on his 1970 trip to China. Reston suffered an attack of appendicitis that required surgery. While Reston's physicians operated, acupuncture was one of the approved anesthesias. The operation was a success and President Nixon arranged for thirty Chinese acupuncturists to visit the United States a few months later (4).

At the very core of the practice of acupuncture is the belief in the balance of yin and yang. Acupuncture and other medicine in China focuses a great deal on the prevention of illnesses. To more fully understand acupuncture, you must consider the current research that suggests that there is a specific relationship between acupuncture points, meridians, and the electrical currents of the body. According to this ancient philosophy, the universe can be described by the dualistic concept of yin and yang. All matter is made of yin and yang, including every part of the human body (Nash 12). Yin is described as that which is dark and cold, while yang is described as that which is light and warm. It is their interaction and balance that creates "a dynamic interplay that we call health." (Kastner, Burroughs 4) Therefore, maintaining various balances can prevent illness and is at the very heart of the practice of preventive medicine through acupuncture. The twelve main meridians are: lungs, large intestine, stomach, spleen, heart, small intestine, bladder, kidney, triple warmer, gallbladder, liver, and gate of life (5).

Achieving balance among these main meridians becomes the basis of preventive medicine and maintenance that is at the heart of acupuncture. Special names are used for the acupuncture points. They can number up to hundreds, but a smaller number of points are used by most practitioners (5).

When a patient visits a qualified acupuncturist in a country such as the United States, the first session is mainly devoted to the acupuncturist listening to the patient. The acupuncturist gets to know the patient through questions and discussion of the person's lifestyle, diet, likes, dislikes, profession, and personal health habits. In other words, the practitioner searches for evidence of disharmony in the patient's life.

When an analysis of the patient's needs is made, the puncture points of the treatment are chosen. Then very fine acupuncture needles are chosen to place under the skin. However, some practitioners use electrical stimulation to these points without the use of needles. Still, patients may feel a tingle from the needle site, but none report any true pain.

This treatment can take up to a half an hour. Again, many patients feel relaxed and agreeable during the treatment. In fact, a sense of euphoria is often reported.

Finally, a schedule for treatment is selected. A patient may continue to visit the acupuncturist for several weeks, with one or two treatments a week, while others may need to continue indefinitely or at least for several months, depending on the reason for seeking therapy in the first place (6).

Usually acupuncture is broken down into two main areas in control of pain. One is the control of pain without medicines and anesthetics during surgical procedures. The second is the control of pain from chronic diseases such as arthritis and back pain. The practitioners do not always see an improvement of the medical condition, but the relief of severe and debilitating pain allows a patient to function and lead a normal life in spite of an otherwise crippling disease.

Western doctors who attended the 1979 Beijing Neuro-surgical Institute in China witnessed major surgery that depend-ed entirely on acupuncture for the relief of the pain during the operation. The patient was having a brain tumor removed. His case is now a documented case where a Chinese neurosurgeon relied on acupuncture as the sole anesthetic. He chose this type of analgesia because it has very few side effects. At the end of the four-hour operation, the patient thanked his surgeon and other medical staff as he walked unassisted out of the operating room.

There are some reports that traditional acupuncture techniques are not always as successful for abdominal surgery. Although most Chinese surgeons rely on acupuncture as an analgesia for operations such as gallbladder removal or appendectomies, there are reports that some doctors are combining acupuncture with Western surgical analgesics for relief of pain.

Individuals with a number of addictions such as smoking, alco-hol dependency, and drugs are now being treated in the United States by acupuncture. The British medical journal *The Lancet* documented a study of the use of acupuncture for addictions in 1989. While acupuncture was used in both Europe and the United States for addictive behavior, this study prepared the way for many medical practitioners to recommend acupuncture to their addicted patients. Dramatic improvements were reported. Although some doctors felt that acupuncture's success could be attributed to a psychological factor more than a physical one, there have been very few studies made to either refute or support the good results. Because addictive behaviors are hard to treat, physicians continue to recommend seeking help through this ancient Chinese medicine.

Another benefit reported is for reducing the effects of ailments such as arthritis, back problems, and rheumatism through acupuncture treatment. In fact, many patients have reported a reversal of these diseases, although medical research has yet to find proof of those reversals. However, many advocates of treatment by acupuncture feel that acupuncture therapy enables a patient to live a more normal life with such treatment (Nash 15).

As with any therapy there are further considerations. For example, Barabara Nash suggests confirming the acupuncturist's licensing through the National Commission for Certification of Acupuncturists (15). Also, she suggests that a patient should expect the acupuncturist to maintain a hygienic place of operation along with medically approved needles. Acupuncturists now use disposable needles. These guidelines serve as a protection to the patient from any harm that could result from the therapy.

Other ways to approach an acupuncturist and the treatment is to avoid therapists who insist on continuing treatment even though the patient is confident that the problem has been alleviated. Any acupuncturist who tries to persuade the patient to leave a traditional medical physician is not interested in the patient, but rather, is pursuing a self-serving practice at the danger of the patient.

In fact, for a patient to choose between acupuncture and accepted medical procedures is a mistake. There are any number of fine doctors who welcome the opportunity to aid and assist their patients in finding an acupuncturist and to follow through on treatment. It is the medical doctor who is in charge of the case as the acupuncturist provides a legitimate adjuvant therapy.

Problems in the use of acupuncture in the United States and

in other countries are a result of deficient practitioners who are giving acupuncture a bad reputation. In some areas, accreditation for the acupuncturist is very poor or completely lacking. Some practitioner's methods are questionable if not harmful. They are allowed to open an office with few restrictions. Therefore, many poorly prepared people are attempting to use acupuncture to make money from unsuspecting, suffering patients.

As a whole, acupuncture is slowly gaining acceptance throughout the world. In the United States, research is taking place. It will be several years before the results of these studies can be evaluated, but the very fact that they are taking place is an acknowledgment that alternative medicines could have a place in modern medicine (Kastner, Burroughs 7). In fact, widespread evidence is being gathered that acupuncture, that ancient Chinese medicine, will become one of the new modern therapies (Nash 15) to be approved and accepted by the most demanding medical practitioners.

Works Cited

Collinge, William. Alternative Medicine. New York: Warner
    Books, Inc., 1996.

Kastner, Mark and Hugh Alternative Healing. LaMesa, CA: Halcyon,
    1993.

Nash, Barbara. From Acupressure to Zen. LaMesa, CA.: Hunter
    House, 1996.

NEW APPLICATIONS FOR AN ANCIENT MEDICINE

Acupuncture is a part of traditional Oriental medicine that is now being studied for its effectiveness as an alternative or adjuvant medical treatment in Western countries as well. With more open communication between China and the United States, and other Western European nations, a sharing of medical knowledge has also taken place. Consequently there is an interest and acknowledgment of some of the successes of acupuncture treatment. In fact, it could be said that since the 1970s there has been an increase in the interest in acupuncture with many new applications for an old medicine.

The name *acupuncture* means to prick with a needle. "It is the art of expertly and painlessly piercing the skin with disposable needles at different points," writes Barbara Nash. What's more, acupuncture, which originated in China, has a history that can be traced back approximately 5,000 years.[1]

However, in the eighteenth and nineteenth centuries, Western patients did not trust the use of needles. This common practice involves using needles for stimulation of the Ho Ku points which in turn causes Teh-ch'i—a tingling sensation that often seems to relieve pain at distant points of the body. This prejudice is said to have prevented the serious study of acupuncture in Western countries. Still, an interest lived on among a handful of medical practitioners. In fact, after years of debate on acupuncture methodology, there are currently several serious efforts to evaluate acupuncture's effectiveness in diagnosing illness, treating illness, managing chronic disorders, relieving pain, and promoting health through prevention and maintenance. [2]

In the United States, acupuncture is receiving special attention as an alternative or adjuvant treatment for many diseases, especially those that are related to the central nervous system or to stress-induced illnesses. But acupuncture remains a vital part of medical practice in contemporary China and other Asian countries. In fact, acupuncture has been the major type of medical treatment there and was only recently integrated with Western medical techniques beginning with nineteenth-century missionaries. However, one of the most dramatic reports of the successful use of acupuncture during a surgical procedure came from James Reston, who accompanied President Nixon on his 1970 trip to China. Reston suffered an attack of appendicitis that required surgery. While Reston's physicians operated, acupuncture was one of the approved anesthesias. The operation was a success and President Nixon arranged for thirty Chinese acupuncturists to visit the United States a few months later. [3]

At the very core of acupuncture is the belief in the balance of yin and yang. Acupuncture and other medicine in China focuses a great deal on the prevention of illnesses. To more fully understand acupuncture, you must consider the current research that suggests that there is a specific relationship between acupuncture points, meridians, and the electrical currents of the body. According to this ancient philosophy, the universe can be described by the dualistic concept of yin and yang. All matter is made up of yin and yang, including every part of the human body.[4]

Yin is described as that which is dark and cold, while yang is described as that which is light and warm. It is their interaction and balance that creates "a dynamic interplay that we call health."[5] Therefore, maintaining balances can prevent illness and is at the very heart of the practice of preventive medicine through acupuncture.

Chinese acupuncture theory maintains that there are twelve main meridians of energy channels running through the body that relate to the internal organs: lungs, large intestine, stomach, spleen, heart, small intestine, bladder, kidney, triple warmer, gallbladder, liver, and gate of life.[6]

Therefore, maintaining a balance among these main meridians becomes the basis of preventive medicine and maintenance that is at the heart of acupuncture. Special names are used for the acupuncture points. They can be numbered up to hundreds, but a smaller number of points are used by most practitioners.[7]

When a patient visits a qualified acupuncturist in a country such as the United States, the first session is mainly devoted the acupuncturist listening to the patient. The acupuncturist gets to know the patient through questions and discussion of the person's lifestyle, diet, likes, dislikes, profession, and personal health habits. In other words, the practitioner searches for evidence of disharmony in the patient's life.

When an analysis of the patient's needs is made, the puncture points of the treatment are chosen. Then very fine acupuncture needles are chosen to place under the skin. (However, some practitioners use electrical stimulation without the use of needles.) Still, patients may feel a tingle from the needle site, but none report any true pain.

This treatment can take up to a half an hour. Again, many patients feel relaxed and agreeable during the treatment. In fact, a sense of euphoria is often reported.

Finally, a schedule for treatment is selected. A patient may continue to visit the acupuncturist for several weeks, with one or two treatments a week, while others may need to continue indefinitely or at least for several months, depending on the reason for seeking therapy in the first place.[8]

Usually, acupuncture is broken down into two main areas in control of pain. One is the control of pain without medicines and anesthesia during surgical procedures. The second is the control of pain of chronic diseases such as arthritis and back pain. Practitioners do not always see an improvement of the medical condition, but the relief of severe and debilitating pain allows a patient to function and lead a normal life in spite of an otherwise crippling disease.

American doctors who attended the 1979 Beijing Neurosurgical Institute in China, witnessed major surgery that depended entirely on acupuncture for the relief of the pain during the operation. The patient was having a brain tumor removed. His case is now a documented case where a Chinese neurosurgeon relied on acupuncture as the sole anesthetic. He chose this type of analgesia because it has very few side effects. At the end of the four-hour operation, the patient thanked his surgeon and other medical staff as he walked unassisted out of the operating room.

There are reports that Chinese surgeons do not always rely completely on acupuncture as an analgesia for operations involving gallbladder removal and other complicated abdominal procedures. The surgeon combines acupuncture with Western analgesics.

Individuals with an addiction such as smoking, alcohol dependency, and drugs are now being treated in the United States by acupuncture. Great Britain has also reported on the use of acupuncture for addictions. A 1989 report prepared the way for medical practitioners to recommend acupuncture to addicted patients elsewhere. Dramatic improvements were reported. Although some doctors felt that acupuncture's success could be attributed to a psychological factor moreso than a physical one, there have been very few studies made to either refute or support these theories. And since addictive behaviors are hard to treat, physicians continue to recommend seeking help through this ancient Chinese medicine.

Another of the uses of acupuncture is for reducing the effects of ailments such as arthritis, back problems, and rheumatism. In fact, many patients have reported a reversal of these diseases, although medical research has yet to find proof of these reversals. But many advocates of treatment by acupuncture feel that acupuncture therapy enables a patient to live a more normal life with such treatment.[9]

As with any therapy, however, there are certain considerations. Barbara Nash suggests confirming the acupuncturist's licensing through the National Commission for Certification for Acupuncturists. Also she suggests that a patient should expect the acupuncturist to maintain a hygienic place for operation along with medically approved needles. Acupuncturists now use disposable needles. These guidelines serve as a protection to the patient from any harm that could result from the therapy.

Other ways to evaluate an acupuncturist and the treatment is to avoid therapists who insist on continuing treatment even though the patient is confident that the problem has been alleviated. Any acupuncturist who tries to persuade a patient to leave a traditional medical physician is not interested in the patient, but rather, is pursuing a self-serving practice at the danger of the patient.

In fact, for a patient to choose between acupuncture and accepted medical procedures is a mistake. There are any number of fine doctors who welcome the opportunity to aid and assist their patients in finding an acupuncturist while following through on conventional treatment. It is the medical doctor who is in charge of the case, as the acupuncturist provides the adjuvant treatment.

Many poor practitioners have set back the use of acupuncture in the United States and in other countries. In some areas, accreditation for acupuncturists is very poor or completely lacking. Their methods are questionable if not harmful, and because they are allowed to open an office with few restrictions many poorly prepared people are attempting to use acupuncture to make money from unsuspecting, suffering patients.

As a whole, acupuncture is slowly gaining acceptance through the world. In the United States, current research is taking place. It will be several years before the results of these studies can be evaluated, but the very fact that they are taking place is an acknowledgment that many alternative medicines may find a place in modern medicine.

In fact, widespread evidence is being gathered that acupuncture, the ancient Chinese medicine of thousands of years, will become one of the new modern therapies to become approved and accepted by the most demanding medical practitioners.

Notes

[1]Barbara Nash, From Acupressure to Zen (Alameda, CA: Hunter House, 1996) 12.

[2]Mark Kastner and Hugh Burroughs, Alternative Healing (La Mesa, CA: Halcyon Publishing, 1993) 4, 5.

[3]Ibid.

[4]Ibid.

[5]Ibid.

[6]Ibid.

[7]Ibid.

[8]Simon Mills and Stephen J. Financo, Alternatives in Healing (New York and Scarborough, Ontario: New American Library, 1989) 14.

[9]Mark Kastner and Hugh Burroughs, Alternative Healing (La Mesa, CA: Halcyon, 1993) 7.

Glossary

The words listed below can be found in the preceding chapters of this book. The definitions are based upon *Merriam Webster's Collegiate Dictionary* (Tenth Edition) and the context in which the word is used.

A

abstracts (n)	Short selections from the original.
academic (adj)	Scholarly.
access (v)	To get at; to get into.
accurate (adj)	Free from errors.
achieve (v)	To complete or to be successful in.
acquire (v)	To come into possession of.
acronym (n)	A word made up from the first letters of a group of words.
acupuncture (n)	Medical healing through stimulation of certain points of one's body.
adapt (v)	To change accordingly.
adequate (adj)	Enough; sufficient.
adopt (v)	To use in a special way.
advantage (n)	A beneficial or a special condition.
advise (v)	To suggest.
affect (v)	To influence.
allow (v)	To permit.
alphabetize (v)	To arrange in sequence by letter.
alter (v)	To change.
alternative (n)	Choice.
analyze (v)	To study in all parts.
ancient (adj)	Having existed many years ago.

apply (v)	To use with purpose.
argue (v)	To attempt to prove something.
arrange (v)	To place in special order.
articles (n)	Short pieces of writing.
assume (v)	To take as factual or true.
attain (v)	To achieve.
attempt (v)	To make an effort.
authority (n)	A trusted source.
available (adj)	Ready to use.
aware (adj)	Knowing what is happening.
awkward (adj)	Not graceful or smooth.
author (n)	The writer.

B

background (n)	Material of lesser but necessary importance.
back matter (n)	Final section of a paper.
bibliography (n)	Alphabetized description of book.
blend (v)	Combine.
body (n)	Middle portion of writing containing examples, facts, illustrations.
brainstorm (v)	To list ideas as they occur.
branch (v)	Arrange by drawing or sketching ideas.
bridge (v)	Joining one part to another.

C

card catalog (n)	File for books according to subject, author, and title.
career (n)	One's life work.
category (n)	A special division or class.
channel (n)	Special electronic pathways.
chronological (adj)	According to date or time.

circulation (n)	To move items from one place to another.
clear (adj)	Easy to understand.
colloquial (adj)	Common place informal speech.
combine (v)	To put together.
communicate (v)	To exchange ideas and feelings with another person.
comparison (n)	To examine two or more things.
compelling (adj)	Important.
compact discs (n)	Small plastic disc with computer data or music.
conclude (v)	To bring to an end.
consistent (adj)	Free of variation and contradiction.
contrast (n)	A comparison of differences.
contribute (v)	To give to or to add.
copyright (n)	Protection against plagiarism.
creative (adj)	Having special and unusual qualities.
credibility (adj)	Believable.
credit (v)	Recognition by name of another author or speaker's ideas.

D

data (n)	Sources of information.
deadline (n)	Date or dates that assignments must be given to instructor.
definition (n)	A statement expressing the meaning of a word.
demand (v)	To make a strong request.
describe (v)	Give special visual, auditory, kinesthetic details.
detail (n)	To communicate information in small units.
determine (v)	To establish ideas.
develop (v)	To expand and increase ideas by adding details and examples.

digress (v)	To ignore the main idea.
direct (v)	To focus attention in a special direction.
distribute (v)	Moving finished material from one person or place to another.
division (n)	Arrangement of material into segments.
domestic (n)	Not foreign.
documentation (n)	Special ways to give credit to others.
draft (n)	Early writing attempts.

E

earn (v)	To achieve something such as money or recognition through special efforts.
edit (v)	To correct and improve writing by changing content, punctuation, sentence structure, etc.
effective (adj)	Producing the desired result.
efficient (adj)	Producing results in the shortest and best manner.
electronic mail (n)	Special messages sent via an electronic network.
element (n)	Part of a whole.
eliminate (v)	To do away with.
emanate (v)	To come from.
emoticons (n)	Computer symbols.
enable (v)	To make possible.
endnotes (n)	List of sources at end of paper.
enhance (v)	To improve.
entitle (v)	To allow.
equal (adj)	Of the same value.
equipment (n)	Machinery that performs special jobs.
error (n)	Mistake.

essay (n)	Form of a written composition.
essential (adj)	Most necessary.
establish (v)	To present a condition or position.
evaluate (v)	To decide upon the merit of materials.
examine (v)	To go over and look at thoroughly.
exchange (v)	To trade one article or condition for another.
expand (v)	To increase or enlarge.
experience (n)	Participation.
expertise (n)	Special skills or knowledge.
export (v)	To supply goods to another country.
express (v)	To communicate by words or symbols.
external (adj)	Referring to outer parts.

F

factor (n)	Contributing element.
familiar (adj)	Well known.
feedback (n)	Reactions to ideas or text.
flexible (adj)	Adaptable to different ideas.
focus (v)	To center attention or group ideas.
footnote (n)	A special note found at the bottom of a page of writing.
force (v)	To make an individual agree or act.
formal (adj)	Orderly or even rigid in character.
format (n)	A special design or arrangement.
fragment (n)	An incomplete sentence.
framework (n)	The basic organization of material.
frequent (adj)	Happening often.
fundamental (adj)	Essential or necessary.
fused (adj)	Connected.

G

gender (n)   Either male or female sex.

gender bias (n)   Bias to one sex or another.

goods (n)   Products that people need.

grammar (n)   The study of what is preferred in syntax and system of language.

guide (v)   To show the way, to give direction.

H

habit (n)   Repetitious activity.

handle (v)   To manage well.

hardware (n)   Physical components of a computer.

high-tech (adj)   Describing advanced technology.

I

ideal (adj)   Referring to the best quality; expectation of certain qualities.

identify (v)   To give meaning to certain matters.

idiom (n)   Words used together to form a special meaning.

implement (v)   To put into action.

import (v)   To bring into one country from another.

inappropriate (adj)   Not suitable.

indent (v)   To allow a certain number of spaces at the beginning of a paragraph, or in an outline format.

independent (adj)   Performed without assistance.

inform (v)   To communicate facts.

insight (n)   An understanding of a relationship or idea.

interpret (v)   To explain.

interview (v)   To seek information through a personal meeting or telephone conversation.

involve (v)   To relate to closely.

irregular (adj)   Not in a regular pattern.

issue (n)   A matter of dispute or a difference.

J

job (n)   An occupation or career.

join (v)   To bring together.

jump (v)   To move suddenly without explanation.

junction (n)   A place where matters join together.

just (adj)   Precisely or with fairness.

justify (v)   To prove correct.

K

keep (v)   To maintain.

key (adj)   Fundamental or main material.

know (v)   To understand or to recall.

knowledge (n)   Information that is capable of being learned.

knowledgeably (adv)   Executed with knowledge.

L

label (n)   An identifying phrase or name.

lack (n)   Deficient, needed.

largely (adj)   Mostly.

last (adj)   The final item of action.

latter (adj)	Relating to the past.
law (n)	Binding rules or legal agreements.
learn (v)	To acquire knowledge and understanding.
likely (adv)	Probably.
limit (v)	To keep within certain conditions.
list (n)	Arrangement.
log (n)	A notebook or list of important facts.
long-term (adj)	Covering a long time.
loose (adj)	Not tightly constructed.
lower (v)	To move down.
luckily (adv)	Fortunately.

M

main idea (n)	Thesis.
maintain (v)	To keep in good working order.
match (v)	To arrange according to similarities.
material (n)	Printed sources or text.
meet (v)	To satisfy certain requirements.
metaphor (n)	An implied likeness.
microfiche (n)	A sheet of microfilm containing rows of images.
microfilm (n)	A photographic record of material.
modem (n)	A device that conveys signals from a computer to a telephone line.

N

narrow down (v)	To bring down in number and scope.
nation (n)	Country.
national (adj)	Characteristic of one nation.

O

objective (n)	Goal.
obtain (v)	To acquire.
omit (v)	To leave out.
on-line database (n)	Data that can be accessed on-line.
operate (v)	To work.
option (n)	Choice.
organization (n)	Groups of people working together.
organizational (adv)	Pertaining to particular organizations.
outline (n)	List of different parts within a certain form.
overall (adv)	In view of all conditions.
overuse (v)	To use too often.

P

paragraph (n)	One or more sentences dealing with one point.
paraphrase (v)	To rewrite into one's own words.
personal (adj)	Not public.
persuasive (adj)	Making an argument to influence.
phrase (n)	Groups of words.
portable database	Data that can be moved from one computer to another.
predetermine (v)	To decide in advance.
present (v)	To give to or to introduce to someone.
primary (adj)	Fundamental.
primary research (n)	Research that is derived from original sources.
prior to (adj)	Before or preceding.
punctuation (n)	Marks in written text that clarify meaning.

Q

quality (adj)   Having characteristics of good or bad features.

quit (v)   To stop doing something.

quite (adv)   To a great extent.

quotation marks (n)   Punctuation used to note quotations.

quote (v)   To mark or to credit words or phrases.

R

reach (v)   Come to a successful point.

recommend (v)   To endorse as reputable.

reflect (v)   To show.

relate to (v)   To connect with.

relative (adj)   Comparative.

restate (v)   To state more than once.

role (n)   Function.

routine (n)   Everyday procedures.

S

schedule (n)   A plan for what is to be done.

sentence outline (n)   An outline prepared in full sentences.

sequence (n)   A series that follows a special order.

share (v)   To reveal or exchange information.

short-term (adj)   Near future.

similar (adj)   Nearly the same.

slang (n)   Informal speech.

software (n)   Something used or associated with hardware.

source (n)   A place where something can be found.

sparingly (adv)   Used with great care in small amounts.

spatial (adj)	Use of space as a coherent writing order.
statistics (n)	Numerical information and data.
stilted (adj)	Stiff, too formal.
strategy (n)	A plan of action.
style (n)	A distinctive manner of expression.
subgrouping (v)	Placing in another group below original.
subordinate (n)	Of lesser importance.
suitable (adj)	To be right for; workable.
summary (n)	A shortened version of the original.
support (v)	To provide details that give credibility.
supportive (adj)	Items and details that support.
symbol (n)	A sign or written element.
symbolize (v)	To provide identification through a sign.

T

take place (v)	To happen.
task (n)	Work that has to be performed.
technology (n)	Scientific and practical knowledge.
temporary (adj)	Not permanent.
thesis (n)	The main idea of a paper.
topic (n)	A subject or discourse of writing.
transition (n)	Smooth connection of ideas.
translate (v)	To express in another language.
turn to (v)	To change direction.

U

unique (adj)	Not of a usual nature.
unusual (adj)	Not ordinary.
usage (n)	Acceptable way words are used in language.

usual (adj)   Of an ordinary appearance or nature.

utilize (v)   To make use of.

V

valid (adj)   Truthful or supported by accurate facts and statistics.

variety (n)   Many different articles or matter.

vary (v)   To use different language or approaches.

view (v)   To observe, to survey.

vital (adj)   Most important.

vulgar (adj)   Inappropriate and without taste.

W

weigh (v)   To consider.

wordiness (n)   Loose construction.

Answer Key to Exercises

CHAPTER ONE

EXERCISE 1: WRITING CONCRETELY

1. Pomeranian
2. Attract
3. Selected
4. Popular

EXERCISE 2: CONQUERING REDUNDANCY—SUGGESTED RESPONSE

1. Better: My neighbor visits her grandmother several times a month.
2. Better: I never read that type of novel.
3. Better: The law intern often works late.

EXERCISE 3: ELIMINATING LOOSE CONSTRUCTION—SUGGESTED RESPONSE

1. Although newly outfitted, the *Titanic* did not have an adequate number of lifeboats.
2. The owners advertised that the *Titanic* was very luxurious and the safest ocean liner ever built.
3. Fifteen hundred passengers and crew drowned that night in 1912, before rescue ships arrived.

EXERCISE 4: FIND THE TRANSITIONS—SUGGESTED RESPONSE

Have you ever thought about what sort of child you were at the age of ten and how it may continue to influence your present life? <u>For instance,</u> were *you an active child who <u>possibly</u> liked to play outdoor games? <u>Perhaps</u> you were a child who enjoyed reading and other quiet pursuits. <u>In other words</u>, most of us have some recollection of our likes and dislikes when we were a certain age. Memories <u>certainly</u> can influence our adult life.*

CHAPTER TWO
EXERCISE 1: WRITING A PROCESS PARAGRAPH—EXAMPLE PARAGRAPH

According to a book written for London housewives in 1608, to preserve whole roses and marigolds, you should dip the buds in a syrup consisting of sugar double refined and rose water boiled for several minutes. Then, the reader was advised, open the leaves of the bud, one by one, with a toothpick. Finally, place them on papers and dry them in the hot sun or in a warm oven.

CHAPTER THREE
EXERCISE 1: PLANNING AN ESSAY—A POSSIBLE RESPONSE

INTRODUCTION
My ideal job would be working for world peace.

BODY
My qualifications for the job: I am multilingual, have a masters degree in liberal arts, and have experience teaching in my country before taking my M.A. in the United States. My interest in teaching would be directed to the middle grades because it is exciting to help young people become aware of the world community and to become instrumental in helping them achieve the background for careers that would impact on world peace. The salary is not the most important aspect of a career, but I would like to have a job that allows me to travel.

CONCLUSION

There may be several types of jobs that might be an ideal one for me. Most important, however, is having a job where I could feel that I am having some impact on world events, no matter how small the scope of my influence.

CHAPTER FOUR

EXERCISE 1: WRITING A THESIS STATEMENT—POSSIBLE RESPONSE

All student teachers, despite their content area, must take a maximum number of credit hours in liberal arts preparation.

Works Cited

American Psychological Association. *Publication Manual of the American Psychological Association.* 4th ed. Washington, DC: Washington American Psychological Assn., 1994.

Gibaldi, Joseph. *MLA Handbook for Writers of Research Papers.* 4th ed. New York: The Modern Language Assn. of America, 1995.

_____. *MLA Style Manual*, 2nd ed. New York: The Modern Language Assn. of America, 1998.

Hitt, A. W. (Tony), and Kurt Wulff. *Positive Impressions: Effective Telephone Skills.* St. Louis, Mo.: Div. of Amer. Inst. of Motivation, 1992.

Longman. *Longman Dictionary of American English.* White Plains, NY: Longman, 1983.

Matthews, Candace, and Joanne Marino. *Professional Interactions Oral Communication Skills in Science, Technology, and Medicine.* Upper Saddle River, NJ: Prentice-Hall, 1990.

McWhorter, Kathleen T. *The Writer's Express: A Paragraph and Essay Text with Readings.* Boston: Houghton Mifflin Co., 1993.

Reinking, James A. and Andrew W. Hart. *Strategies for Successful Writing, A Rhetoric, Reader, and Handbook.* Englewood Cliffs, NJ: Prentice-Hall, 1991.

Skilkin, Marjorie E. *Words into Type.* Englewood Cliffs, NJ: Prentice-Hall, 1974.

Strunk, Jr., William and White, E. B. *The Elements of Style.* 3rd ed. New York: The Macmillan Co., 1959.

Troyka, Lynn Quitman. *Simon and Schuster Handbook for Writers.* 2nd ed. Upper Saddle River, NJ: Prentice-Hall, Inc., 1993.

Turabian, Kate L. *A Manual for Writers of Term Papers, Theses, and Dissertations.* 5th ed. Chicago, IL: The University of Chicago Press, 1987.

Suggested Reading

Berka, Roy M., Andrew D. Wolvin, and Darlyn R. Wolvin. *Communicating*, 5th ed. Boston: Houghton Mifflin Co., 1992.

Donald, Robert B., *Writing Clear Paragraphs*, 4th ed. Englewood Cliffs, NJ: Prentice-Hall, 1991.

Gibaldi, Joseph, *MLA Style Manual and Guide to Scholarly Publishing*, 2nd ed. New York: The Modern Language Association, 1998.

Leeds, Bruce, Editor, *Writing in a Second Language*, Boston: Addison-Wesley, 1996.

Legett, Glenn, C. David Mead, and Melinda G. Kramer. *Prentice-Hall Handbook for Writers*, 11th ed. Englewood Cliffs, NJ: Prentice-Hall, 1991.

Troyka, Lynn Quitman and Jerrold Nudelman. *Steps in Composition*, 5th ed. Upper Saddle River, NJ: Prentice-Hall, 1990.

Index